THE UNSEEN PROVIDENCE

Inspired by true events.

Written by: Theresa A. Fuller

Copyright © 2012

Jackson J. Fuller

This story was written in memory of:

My great-great grandfather
Rev. Carolina Fuller

And

His son, my great-grandfather,

Jackson J. Fuller

Jackson J. Fuller

1852 - 1919

ACKNOWLEDGEMENTS

I am indebted to the following people for their support:

To my friend and mentor, John Rosati, thank you for all of your support.

To my cousin, Sherman Houston, thank you for all of your support.

To my friend, Marc Libidinsky, thank you for all of your support.

To Lloyd Williams who photographed the church and cemetery, thank you.

In memory of
Shirley Jean Fuller-Green

She is greatly missed. I appreciate her impeccable research and records of the Fuller's history that facilitated the writing of this book.

Jackson J. Fuller

CONTENTS

Jackson J. Fuller

CONTENTS (cont'd.)

AUTHOR'S PREFACE

As a child, I often times heard my father talk about his grandpa Jackson. I was too young to realize that the man he was talking about was someone famous throughout the state of Louisiana and other parts of the south. Of course, to my father, he was just grandpa. My father only remembered the most basic facts about him because he was five years old when Grandpa Jackson died. The stories that he told me and my siblings were told to him by his father, Carolina Fuller, Grandpa Jackson's son.

I grew up feeling like I knew my great grandfather, Jackson. I always felt a spiritual connection to him and didn't know why until now. As a child, I use to pray to God and ask him to let me be close to him as my great grandpa Jackson was. At that time, I was too young to realize what I was asking. I had no idea that when much is given, much is required.

In July 2011, I went to Kingston, Louisiana outside of Shreveport for a family reunion that consisted of only Jackson's and Harriett's descendants. There were approximately 500 of us in attendance (approximately, 300 were absent), and we had a great time. It took place at Mt. Mariah Baptist Church, the first church that Grandpa Jackson's father, Rev. Carolina Fuller built in 1860. The original church has long since been demolished. A new worship sanctuary and offices have been constructed. Mt. Mariah Baptist Church is one of the most beautiful and elegant churches in Louisiana. It is a wealthy (spiritually and financially) and vibrant place of worship for hundreds of people. Inside the church, I felt a connection to both grandfathers, Rev. Carolina and Bishop Jackson. Its ambiance made me feel as though I was experiencing a touch of heaven.

When I went on the tour to see land that Grandpa Jackson had purchased over 100 years ago, I was riding with 50 others in a wagon, and what I saw was overwhelming. As far as my eyes could see, there was so much land. I thought to myself. "A former slave, a black man, owned all of this during a time when most whites didn't." There were countless trees on the land being sold for manufacturing paper. Also, there were gas and oil derricks in view with oil trucks driving fast in every direction. I felt like I was in a movie. Today, the Fullers who didn't sell their land over the years are living wealthy lives from their profits and royalties.

After the tour, I attended the BBQ. It was there I visualized Grandpa Jackson, at age five, standing on a plantation wearing short pants and no shoes. I felt as if I had traveled back in time. I was hesitant to share this vision until the next day, because I didn't quite understand what I had experienced.

Jackson J. Fuller

While on the returned airplane trip to California, it occurred to me why I had the vision and why I felt compelled to go to the reunion in Louisiana. My mind became filled with thoughts of writing a book and screenplay about my grandfathers, Rev. Carolina and Bishop Jackson Fuller. Several weeks later, I found myself writing a screenplay. All of the scenes appeared to me as though I was watching television. Again, I felt as though I was taken back in time. My emotions changed like a kaleidoscope while writing the screenplay. The scenes had me angry, sad, laughing and rejoicing. You name it - I was experiencing it. The screenplay was completed within eight weeks. A few months later, I was inspired to write this book.

Writing this book was gratifying and inspirational. The research enriched me with much knowledge about these two great men. I learned that Christopher Columbus, my great-great-great grandfather, Rev. Carolina's father, was the first of my ancestors to come bound in chains to America from Africa. His descendants, Carolina and Jackson were born into slavery for purposes that were oblivious to them and to their master. Their experiences were truly an unseen providence that would become clear through their lives. After writing this book, I clearly understand when and why providence was prevalent in this saga.

Jackson J. Fuller

Jesse Fuller
1914 – 1989

He is my father, Grandpa Jackson's grandson, and the son of Carolina and Annie Fuller.

Jackson J. Fuller

1852 - 1919

INTRODUCTION

It's 1852 and slaves are escaping by the hundreds. Slave masters are desperate to catch them or kill them.

Master Wade, a cruel and ruthless plantation slave owner, has only 30 slaves left after 40 escaped. He's determined to keep his remaining slaves from escaping. What he doesn't know is that Carolina, his slave overseer, is a preacher who can read, write, and is spiritually receiving visions from God that are preparing him and Master Wade's other slaves to escape to freedom. Carolina's best friend, a white man named Joshua, taught him how to read and write when they were children. Joshua and Carolina met when they were eight years old at a pond deep in the woods. They met regularly and bonded as brothers. Now grown, Carolina is a preacher and secretly preaches to the other slaves in the woods under a "brush arbor." Joshua stands guard with his shot gun and dog watching for any white intruders. He owns a farm one mile from Master Wade's plantation.

Rev. Carolina – age 38 has a wife named Patsy – age 35, three boys named Aaron age - 10, Stuart – age 8, Jackson – age 5, and one daughter name Dilsie – age 9. All of the children are extremely smart. Jackson is different from the other children. He's young in age and has the mind of an old soul. Like his father, he has true dreams and visions.

Master Wade is desperate for money and decides to take Jackson to be auctioned. Rev. Carolina and his family can do nothing but watch Master Wade take him away. During the bidding, Jackson is the only boy on the block to be sold. A young slave woman is standing protectively close to Jackson. Master DuBois, an anonymous abolitionist, bids $600 for each, Jackson and the young slave woman. This is very unusual. The auctioneer is shocked by such a high bid and quickly yells, "SOLD." Jackson is sold into freedom and doesn't even know it. He's taken far away from South Carolina to Louisiana. One year later, the abolitionist helps Jackson's family escape from the plantation in South Carolina and reunites them with Jackson in Louisiana.

It's 1860, five years prior to the 1865 "Emancipation Proclamation." Jackson is now eight years old and is attending classes taught by an educated black couple. He is eager to learn as much as he can and walks eight miles each day to be taught. His favorite book is the Bible. While attending classes, he meets a younger girl named Harriett who he believes will one day be his wife.

Rev. Carolina has finished building the first former-slaves' church called Mt. Mariah Baptist Church in Kingston, Louisiana. In freedom, he and his wife

Patsy have had two additional children, Jesse and Irene. A few years later, Rev. Carolina successfully builds two more churches within DeSoto Parish named New Bethlehem Baptist Church and Antioch Baptist Church.

In 1871, at the age of 19, Jackson marries Harriett Johnson. Rev. Carolina and Patsy give them land; and, Jackson's brothers help build their house. In 1886, at the age of 71 Rev. Carolina dies after being the pastor of Mt. Mariah Baptist Church for 26 years. Jackson is 34 years old and is the Pastor of Bethlehem Baptist Church. Shortly, after his father's death, he is appointed Pastor of Mt. Mariah Baptist Church and later becomes Bishop over 30 churches throughout DeSoto Parish. During this time, hundreds of people are being saved and baptized through his ministry. His reputation as a spiritual leader spreads throughout the black and white communities. His life is truly becoming an extraordinary phenomenon during this difficult "post-slavery" era.

Many dangerous obstacles are present in Jackson's path, but nothing can stop him from reaching his destiny. He has purchased more than 860 acres of land enriched with gas and oil. The Fuller's ranch is one of the most profitable ranches in DeSoto Parish. It is well known for its crops' high production profits and for providing free food to the poor. Jackson is busy establishing accredited schools at every black church throughout DeSoto Parish for black children to become educated.

As time progresses, Jackson and Harriett now have 14 grown children. They have nine (9) sons and five (5) daughters. The sons are: John, Charlie, Dudley, Carolina, Primus, Jesse, Rochelle, Ernest and Clifton. The daughters are: Alice, Irene, Dilsie, Mimie and Gracie. All five daughters have gone to college and are teachers. Clifton, the youngest son goes to college to become a teacher. After he graduates, he changes his mind about teaching and becomes a train conductor. The other sons take care of the ranch.

In 1896, ten years after Rev. Carolina's death, his friend Joshua is discovered living on land owned by Jackson's son, Dudley. Joshua has no idea whose land he has settled on far into the woods. He left South Carolina during the war when his farm was burned to the ground and after his wife died. He came to Louisiana looking for his friend, Rev. Carolina and doesn't know that he's dead.

Jackson is hated by the Klansmen. They made two attempts to kill him and failed. Their last attempt resulted in devastation for them. This incident was strange and caused the Klansmen to fear him.

In 1915, Jackson's wife Harriett dies from liver cancer and heart failure. Harriett was the love of his

1852 - 1919

life. Her death has him heavily troubled. In 1916, one year after Harriett's death, Jackson meets and gets engaged to a woman named Elida Green. Shortly after being married, they have two children one year apart. In 1919, three years after being married to Elida, Jackson dies from a massive heart attack. While hundreds of people attend his funeral, the Klansmen rejoice over his death.

In 1930, eleven years later, the KKK decides to target another Fuller man. They focus on Jackson's son, Jesse. Jesse is being driven by his chauffeur in his new 1930 Rolls Royce-Hudson when the Klansmen kill him, and makes it look like an accident.

Today, in 2012, Jackson's legacy continues to be talked about throughout the south.

1852 - 1919

**Bishop Jackson J. Fuller
"A Preacher Man Not To
Be Reckoned With"**

CHAPTER 1

THE MASTER PLAN TO ESCAPE SLAVERY

IT'S EARLY MORNING IN THE WOODED SWAMP AREA OF COLUMBIA, SOUTH CAROLINA. TIRED AND WEAK, SLAVES ARE FRANTICALLY RUNNING THROUGH THE SWAMPS WHILE WHITE MEN AND THEIR BARKING DOGS CHASE THEM. AS THEY STRUGGLE THROUGH THE MARSH LAND, SOME ARE KILLED WITH SHOT GUNS.

Master John Wade is traveling, at a fast pace, through the country side of Columbia, South Carolina. He's wearing a pin-striped suit and wide brim hat. He has just left a meeting held with other plantation owners where they discussed what to do about stopping their slaves from escaping. Slaves are escaping by the hundreds using the underground-railroad network. Many are headed north and some to other states to find their families who were sold away from them.

Saddled on the back of a beautiful black horse, Master Wade rides towards his plantation. He's concerned about his cotton crops being cultivated before the winter, because more than 40 of his slaves have fled to freedom. While riding down a two mile tree-lined road leading to his two story white mansion, he turns aside to go towards the cotton field where his remaining 30 slaves tiresomely sweat and chop cotton.

Master John Wade angrily yells, "Carolina! Why in the hell are all of you niggers standing there doing nothing? Don't you realize that we are shorthanded and these goddamn cotton fields must be chopped by the end of the month?" Rev. Carolina is age 38. He answers, "Yes sir, master – it will be done, sir. I'll see to it. We'll get it done." Rev. Carolina is not afraid of Master Wade. He's speaking with confidence and is looking him directly into his eyes. Master Wade doesn't say another word. He stares at Rev. Carolina and turns, riding his horse towards his house. Rev. Carolina's wife, Patsy is age 35, and she's working next to him. She whispers, "How do you suppose we can do so much in such little time?" Rev. Carolina calmly looks at her and says, "God will make a way. Have faith."

Their five year old son, Jackson, is extremely smart and often time he sees visions. He stops chopping the cotton and looks at his pa. "Pa, if you say we can do it – then I believe we can. Ma, believe that we can do it." Patsy is amazed at what he said. She looks at him smiling, "Son, as young as you are, I sometime believe that you have an old man living in your little body. (She shakes her head and laughs.) Lord, the words that come out of his mouth!"

Aaron is ten years old and is listening as he continues to chop the cotton. "Pa, I don't believe we can do what you say can be done. Even though the master won't agree – we are not animals. Jackson! Sometimes you're smart. But, sometimes I wonder how can you think the way you do? You think everything can be done."

Dilsie, nine years old, is chopping cotton in the row next to Jackson and her ma. She has nothing to say. Her brother, Stuart, is eight years old. He's looking at her wondering why she's so quiet. "Dilsie! Did you swallow your tongue? You always have something to say." Rev. Carolina stops chopping cotton and looks at the children, "No more talk. There is a lot of work that needs to be done."

MASTER WADE'S SLAVE QUARTERS HAVE 70 CABINS. IT IS LOCATED IN A CLEARING APPROX. 100 FT. FROM DENSE TREES AND ONE MILE FROM JOSHUA'S FARM; A PLACE WHERE REV. CAROLINA, COVERED IN "SKUNK OIL," SNEAKS AWAY TO LATE AT NIGHT TO LEARN ABOUT THE UNDERGROUND-RAILROAD.

REV. CAROLINA'S ONE ROOM CABIN IS BIGGER THAN MOST. IT HAS SLEEPING AREAS THAT ARE SEPARATED BY HANGING HAND-MADE QUILTS. THE

FAMILY IS SITTING AT A BIG WOODEN TABLE HAVING DINNER.

Rev. Carolina is sitting at the head of the table eating and talking with his family. He's anxious to tell them some exciting news. "Everybody, listen closely to what I'm about to say. Things are getting bad. Slaves are escaping to the north by the hundreds. Some masters are giving them papers to become free because they can't afford to keep them. There are not many of us left to do the work. God has shown me another vision. Time is near for us to be leaving Master Wade. Joshua is working on making this happen. To prevent the hunting dogs from following us, I want all of you to prepare enough "skunk oil" to cover yourselves with and everything we leave behind. We can't afford for the dogs to have our scents. Don't say a word about this to nobody."

Jackson adds, "Pa, I had a vision too. I saw you and ma hiding and running through the trees heading towards a place called Louez." Squinting her eyes, Patsy is looking at Jackson, "Son, you must be talking about Louisiana. God sure is showing you. You don't know a thing about Louisiana. Aaron, what do you think about all this?" Aaron, speaking with excitement in his voice responds, "How soon do you think we can leave?" Looking at her Pa, Dilsie grimly says, "The sooner - the better. Pa, I don't like being a slave. I don't like Master Wade. He's a bad man. He calls us nigger every time he comes around." Stuart is very excited too and adds, "Amen to that. I can't wait to be free. When can we go Pa?" Rev. Carolina answers, "As soon as God makes it clear to me that it's time. Nobody knows better than him. Jackson, I believe God is going to use you in a mighty way. He has blessed you with wisdom that not many your age has got. All of you children are smart. Now, come Sunday on our day of rest from the fields, we're going to secretly meet with the others under the "Brush Arbor" to worship God. That's when I'm going to share the vision. They'll be excited to know that our deliverance is soon."

IT'S SUNDAY MORNING AT THE WOODED AREA BEHIND THE SLAVE QUARTERS. MASTER WADE'S SLAVES ARE STANDING UNDER A "BRUSH ARBOR." EVERY MAN, WOMAN, AND CHILD IS DRESSED IN THEIR SUNDAY BEST, LISTENING TO REV. CAROLINA. JOSHUA, CAROLINA'S WHITE FRIEND, IS STANDING GUARD WITH HIS RIFLE AND DOG TO MAKE SURE NO WHITE INTRUDERS ARE NEARBY. HE AND CAROLINA HAVE BEEN FRIENDS SINCE THEY WERE CHILDREN.

Rev. Carolina has a Bible in his hand, and he's wearing a suit that Patsy made. He's standing in front of 24 slaves who are sitting on logs waiting to hear him preach. With a serious look on his face, he begins to speak, "You all know, there is no God like God Almighty. All power is in his hands and a band of angels are about us at all times. The day is very near for God to deliver us and set us free. We have got to believe and keep talking to him. We are not animals, and our children are not animals. We are not to be hung from trees, skinned like hogs, and beaten like mules. We are God's children, and he is going to set all of us free soon, soon, soon. If you want to go to freedom, it is time to start preparing and be ready when the time comes for us to leave. Be sure to make enough "skunk Oil" to cover yourselves and all of your belongings that you leave behind. Like a thief in the night, our escape will be just that way. We must travel light. All provisions will be made for us along the way. Amen."

1852 - 1919

CHAPTER 2

AGE 5 – JACKSON SOLD INTO FREEDOM

It's early, 5:00 a.m., three days after Rev. Carolina's sermon. Master Wade is standing in front of Carolina's cabin banging loudly on the door and yelling his name, "Carolina! Carolina!" Rev. Carolina rushes to open the door with a curious look on his face. "Good morning, sir. What can I do for you so early?" Master Wade speaks nervously with trembling lips, "I have some bad news. I'm here to take Jackson to be sold. It's something that I've got to do. I'm losing lots of money because of runaway slaves; and, I can get a good amount by selling Jackson. He's young, but he's smart and motivated. He'll grow up to be valuable."

Patsy, standing behind Rev. Carolina begins screaming and is holding on tightly to Jackson. She moves towards the door of the cabin in front of Rev. Carolina and angrily yells at Master Wade, "You can't take my baby. He's only five years old. How can you take him from his mama? What kind of a man are you? You can't have him." Rev. Carolina, with rage in his voice, moves Patsy and Jackson aside and gets very close to Master Wade as he steps back startled. He yells, "Master, take me – not my boy. How can you take my young boy from me?" Aaron, Dilsie, and Stuart are standing motionless with tears running down their faces. Jackson, trying to be brave, pulls away from his ma. He goes to his pa and looks up at him, saying in a confident voice, "Pa! I'll be alright." He kisses his ma and hugs each one of them. As he walks away from the cabin, he looks back and says, "Pa, remember Louez." He gets into the wagon with Master Wade and doesn't look back.

SLAVE AUCTION – THERE ARE MANY SLAVES IN CHAINS (MEN AND WOMEN) STANDING ON THE AUCTION BLOCK TO BE SOLD. JACKSON IS THE ONLY CHILD AND IS STANDING IN THE FRONT.

The auctioneer begins bidding, "This boy is young, but he's smart and strong. He's going to be a good worker when he's older. The bid starts at $200." Jackson is standing straight with no shirt on as he looks ahead not making eye contact with the bidders. Master DuBois, an anonymous abolitionist from Louisiana is staring at Jackson and the lady standing behind him. He's thinking a boy so young shouldn't be away from his folks. Again, the auctioneer yells out "$200.00." Master DuBois quickly bids, "I'll pay $600.00 for the boy and $600.00 for the young lady standing behind the boy." The auctioneer is stunned by such high bids. He quickly accepts the bids for Jackson and the woman. He shouts, "Sold for $600.00 each, the boy and the woman behind him."

1852 - 1919

Master DuBois is approaching the auction block to get Jackson and the woman. All of the bidders watch Master DuBois closely as he approaches the auction block to get Jackson and the woman. He speaks to Jackson and the young woman in an unfriendly tone, "My name is Master Dubois. I'll be taking you to my plantation in Shreveport, Louisiana. Come with me." Jackson and the young woman step down from the auction block and walk behind Master DuBois to a beautiful large carriage. There standing is a black man dressed in a strange looking suit that has long tails hanging. He is wearing a tall hat and has a big grin on his face as he opens the door for them to get in. Jackson and the young woman are very nervous about being inside of a carriage with a new Master who has spoken to them so unpleasantly at the auction. They don't know what to expect from this white man who is looking at them with no expression on his face. Finally, he looks only at Jackson, "What's your name boy?" Jackson is slow to answer as he thinks about the Louez vision, "Ah, sir, my name is Jackson and I'm five years old." Master DuBois stops staring at him and looks at the young woman, "What is your name?" The young woman answers with a beautiful accent, "I'm Sadie." She doesn't make eye contact with him. Master Dubois is sensing how uncomfortable Jackson and Sadie appear to be, and he shifts to a different position in his seat. Now, he speaks in a very pleasant voice, "It's a pleasure to know you both." He extends his hand to Sadie for a hand shake and then to Jackson as he asks, "Jackson, who all did you leave behind?" Jackson, noticing the pleasantness in his voice, felt more comfortable, "Sir, I had to leave my pa, my ma, my sister Dilsie, and my brothers Aaron and Stuart." With a sympathetic voice, Master Dubois responds, "Well, I know it's difficult, with you being so young and all, to be taken away from your family. Maybe one day, you all will be together again. Nothing is impossible." Hearing this, Jackson smiles at him and says, "Sir, I hope so. I believe God can make anything happen."

Master DuBois smiles at Sadie and asks, "Did you leave family behind?" No longer afraid to look at him, she answers, "No sir, I don't have any brothers or sisters, and my ma and pa were hung because they took food from the Master's kitchen." Teary eyed, she looks away from Master DuBois. Feeling Sadie's pain, he responds with sadness in his voice, "Sadie, I'm sorry to hear that. Can you cook?" She looks at him, "Sir, I'm one of the best." Master DuBois nods and says, "Good. I want you to work in my kitchen. You and Jackson will never be hungry for food again. Jackson? You seem very smart and I like you. Sadie, I want you to look after Jackson as though he were your son. Jackson, you won't have to work the fields. You're too young for that. You can water and take care of the flowers around the plantation and help Sadie as she sees fit. Now, we have far to travel. From looking at the two of you, I believe you can use some food, new clothes, and a

1852 - 1919

bath. When we get to the next town, I'll get you some food, clothing, and then we'll find a place for the two of you to wash up and get changed." Jackson and Sadie have never experienced such kindness from a master and look at each other with a questioning look.

CHAPTER 3

THE PERFECT ESCAPE

NINE MONTHS LATER. JOSHUA'S BARN. REV. CAROLINA, JOSHUA, AND SLAVES FROM NEARBY PLANTATIONS ARE SECRETLY MEETING TO PLAN AN ESCAPE.

Joshua stands in front of at least 40 slaves who are sitting inside his barn on stacks of hay waiting to learn about the next under-ground railroad escape. He speaks, "Attention, I have something very important to say. I've heard from a leader of the slave freedom movement in Louisiana. He's sending someone here to the farm to lead the next group of slaves to freedom - in Louisiana. Those of you who are ready to go must be here at midnight next Sunday. No one can be late or you'll be left behind. The journey to Louisiana will be dangerous and difficult. With God willing, you'll make it to freedom. Now, go home and don't act any differently. Don't give anybody a reason to become suspicious." Hearing the mention of Louisiana, Rev. Carolina yells, "Louisiana? So be it." He speaks in a lower voice to himself. "Jackson, son you sure saw a true vision from God - Louisiana! God surely works in mysterious ways."

After the meeting, Rev. Carolina and Joshua stand outside the barn. Rev. Carolina is so happy about the

Louisiana news that he hugs Joshua and says, "Joshua, you've been my best friend since we were little boys. When we first met at the pond, I didn't know that you'd be the one to teach me how to swim, how to read; and, now you've made a way for me and my family to become free. I love you my friend and may the good Lord always keep you safe." Joshua laughs and tries to pull away from Rev. Carolina's bear hug. He's yells. "Carolina! Carolina! Let me go. You're getting that "skunk oil" all over me. I'm happy you'll be free so you won't have to drown yourself in that stink oil anymore. You're getting it all over me. Let me go." Rev. Carolina removes his arms from around Joshua and says, "Okay, Joshua. I've got to go and tell the family the good news. See you Sunday night." He runs off into the woods and heads back to his cabin.

It's 2:00 A.M. – WOODED AREA BETWEEN THE SLAVE QUARTERS AND JOSHUA'S FARM. REV. CAROLINA RUNS FAST THROUGH THE WOODS THANKING GOD FOR DELIVERING HIM AND HIS FAMILY TO FREEDOM. HE HAS A VISION AS HE HEADS TOWARDS HIS CABIN; HE IS BUILDING CHURCHES IN LOUISIANA - NO MORE "BRUSH ARBOR." HE SEES HIMSELF STANDING IN A REAL PULPIT IN A CHURCH AND JACKSON IS THERE.
3:00 A.M. – SLAVE QUARTERS.

Rev. Carolina rushes into his cabin, and speaks with a loud whisper, "Everybody wake up! Wake up! We are leaving next Sunday night to go to Louisiana. We're going to be free. We're going to go find Jackson." He falls to his knees and starts thanking God for the freedom that's coming. Suddenly, he stops and there's a moment of silence. He asks, "Lord, since we are going be free, what should our last name be?" I will not be called by Master Wade's name." He reaches for his Bible, quickly turns the pages and reads out loud, "**Mark 9:3 After six days, Jesus takes with him Peter, John and James and leads them up into a high mountain apart by themselves and he transfigured before them. His raiment became shining, exceedingly white as snow. So as no FULLER on earth can white them.**" He closes the Bible, shuts his eyes for a second and says, "**Fuller**! Our new name is **Fuller**." He begins to praise God with an African praise dance. His pa, Christopher Columbus, who came to America from Africa taught him the dance.

11:00 P.M. SUNDAY NIGHT REV. CAROLINA'S CABIN. THE FAMILY PREPARES TO ESCAPE AND COVERS THEMSELVES WITH "SKUNK OIL." THEY POUR OIL OVER EVERYTHING THAT'S BEING LEFT BEHIND TO GET RID OF THEIR SCENTS.

Rev. Carolina is dressed and ready to start the long journey to Louisiana to find his son. He and his family are covered with "skunk oil." As they gather their few belongings to take with them, he heads towards the door of the cabin saying, "Hurry up. The others will be waiting just inside the woods. We can't be late." Patsy, excited about leaving, assures the children that everything is going to be alright, "Children we have a long dangerous journey ahead. Know that God will be with us. We are going to go to Louisiana and find your brother, Jackson." They all go quickly to the woods behind the slave quarters and meet the other slaves who are escaping from Master Wade's plantation. All of them are covered with "skunk oil." As they run quickly towards Joshua's farm, Rev. Carolina leads the way.

CLOSE TO MIDNIGHT – SUNDAY – JOSHUA'S BARN. JOSHUA AND THE SLAVE FREEDOM MOVEMENT LEADER WAIT FOR THE SOON-TO-BE FREE SLAVES.

The freedom leader and Joshua stand outside the barn waiting for their arrival. The freedom leader is ready to leave as Rev. Carolina and the slaves approach. He anxiously says, "Listen up everybody! We are going to be moving fast. You all must be quiet on this journey. We don't want anyone to hear us. What is that smell? Whatever it is should keep the hunting dogs from finding us. It stinks and it was a good idea. There will be people along the way to feed and clothe all of you. It won't be an easy journey, but it will be worth your while. You all will get papers saying you're free as we get closer to Louisiana." Joshua is sad to see Rev. Carolina leave him; yet, he's happy that he's going to freedom. Walking towards Rev. Carolina, he begins to speak, "It's clear. No one is out tonight looking for runaways. Y'all better leave now. Carolina! God be with you. I hope to see you again." He hugs his friend and watches all of them run towards the swamps.

Rev. Carolina and his family are behind the freedom leader; and, the others follow close behind. As they struggle through the swamps, some fall while others pick them up. No one is to be left behind; some of the younger children are being carried. The freedom leader constantly looks back at them and urges, "Keep moving. It's not too far ahead before we get to better conditions."

8:00 A.M. THE NEXT MORNING – MASTER WADE'S PLANTATION. EIGHT HOURS AFTER THE ESCAPE, MASTER WADE RIDES OUT TO THE CROPS TO CHECK ON REV. CAROLINA AND THE SLAVES. FROM A DISTANCE, HE DOESN'T SEE ANYONE WORKING IN THE FIELDS; SO, HE STOPS AND HEADS TOWARDS THE SLAVES' QUARTERS.

1852 - 1919

Master Wade rides his horse to Rev. Carolina's cabin. He gets off the horse and walks up to the door and opens it. Entering the cabin, he notices everything is tossed and smells like skunk. Angrily, he yells out, "Damn you Carolina! You've run away with all of my slaves. When I find you, I'm going to hang you in the presence of your family and everybody else." He gets on his horse and rushes back to his house to recruit a posse to find them.

AT MASTER WADE'S PLANTATION, THE POSSE OF WHITE MEN WITH THEIR DOGS ARE EAGER TO GET STARTED. MASTER WADE HAS A HIGH PRICE ON CAROLINA'S HEAD.

Master Wade stands on his porch and speaks angrily to the posse, "I want y'all to find those black ass niggers and bring them back. I'll pay $100 for each slave that you catch. Their leader's name is Carolina. Bring him back alive if you can; I'll pay $300 to whoever catches him. The escape was his idea. I want to hang that nigger. If you have to kill him, bring me his body. I want to see him dead. They have a good start ahead of you, so don't be slow about it. Take the dogs to the slave quarters and let them sniff around to get all of their scents."

In the slave quarters, the dogs go in and out of every cabin sniffing to find a scent. The leader of the posse stays on his horse watching them while smoking a cigar. Finally, he yells out to the men, "Stop searching! Those niggers were smart. They managed to get rid of their scents. We won't be able to find them. Mr. Wade is going to be very disappointed. He has lost a lot of money losing those slaves. Hell, he'll probably lose his crops and everything else. Let's go back and tell him that there's nothing we can do about those runaways."

CHAPTER 4

FREEDOM IN LOUISIANA

ONE YEAR LATER.

REV. CAROLINA HAS SETTLED IN THE RURAL AREA OF LOUISIANA. HE LEARNS WHERE JACKSON IS LIVING.

Rev. Carolina and several of his friends head towards DuBois's plantation to negotiate a deal for Jackson's freedom. Master DuBois sits on the porch smoking a cigar as they ride up to the plantation house. Rev. Carolina speaks first, "Morning sir, my name is Carolina Fuller." Master DuBois asks in return, "How can I help you men?" Rev. Carolina gets off of his horse, and as he steps onto the porch he answers, "Master Dubois, sir, I'm here to talk to you about my boy, Jackson. He is seven years old, and was sold away from me two years ago in South Carolina. I heard that he lives here on your plantation. Sir, we've come to make a deal with you. Your crops are in need of work and that tells me that you don't have enough slaves. My friends and I will work your crops for the next four months free in exchange for Jackson's freedom. I want my boy home with his family." Master DuBois pretends that he's shocked about Rev. Carolina's arrival and says, "Well now, it's mighty bold of you coming here with such a proposition. You said your name is

Carolina? How long have you been here in Louisiana?" Rev. Carolina responds, "Sir, I've been here one year now." Master Dubois wants to let Jackson go home with his father immediately, but he can't because it might seem too obvious that he's an abolitionist. He thinks a while how he might negotiate Jackson's freedom without divulging his true identity. After a few moments, he speaks calmly to Carolina, "Well now, because you've boldly come here to ask for your son in exchange for free labor, I'm going to say yes. You can have your boy, Jackson, for two months of free labor instead of four. You men don't need to work a full day. I will only require four hours per day of your time." Rev. Carolina and his friends rejoice at the deal, and they rush to shake Master DuBois's hand. Anxious to see Jackson, Rev. Carolina asks. "Sir, if it's not asking too much, can I see my boy? It's been a long time." Master DuBois politely answers, "I can't see any harm in you visiting with your boy. The slave quarters are down that road about one half mile. He's cared for by a woman named Sadie. She stays in the 3rd cabin on the left as you enter the quarters."

Master DuBois stands on the porch watching as Rev. Carolina and his friends ride away toward the slave quarters. He feels good about Jackson and his father being together again, and he laughs and says out loud to himself, "I wish I can see little Jackson's face when he sees his pa. This reunion calls for a glass of wine even if it is early morning. Carolina must never know that I arranged his escape to come to Louisiana to get his boy."

DUBOIS SLAVE QUARTERS – CABIN WHERE JACKSON LIVES WITH SADIE

Rev. Carolina and his friends ride their horses to the slave quarters; headed for the third cabin on the left where Jackson and Sadie live. He gets off his horse and quickly goes up to the door and knocks. Sadie opens the door dressed in her usual attire, a colorful head bandana and matching dress. She has a curious look on her face as she cautiously addresses him, "What you want?" Rev. Carolina, admiring her beautiful accent, introduces himself, "Ma'am, I'm Jackson's pa, and I'm here to see my boy." Jackson, hearing his pa's voice, runs around Sadie and into his pa's arms. He excitedly says, "Pa, you found me. I knew you'd come." Rev. Carolina kneels down and hugs Jackson as tightly as he can and says, "I'm here son. Your ma, Aaron, Stuart, and Dilsie are here too." He holds Jackson away from him to tell him some more good news, "Guess what? You've got a new little brother named Jesse who's waiting to meet you. I've had a talk with Master DuBois about taking you home. In two months, I'll be able to do just that after I finish some work for him. Until then, I'll be here every day to see you. In two months, son, you'll be home with the family."

Jackson beams and excitedly responds, "Okay! I'm going help you work. Pa, I'm so happy. Tell ma, Aaron, Dilsie, Stuart and my new brother, Jesse, that I love them. Pa, I always pray to God and he's giving me lots of visions. I keep seeing you preaching in a real church, a white church." Rev. Carolina laughs and says, "Son, you sure know what you're seeing. God gave me the same vision. I'm talking with some men folks about building a church. The time is coming soon to stop preaching under the "Brush Arbor." I've got to go now, and I'll see you tomorrow." He kisses Jackson on the forehead and stands. He turns to Sadie and says, "Ms. Sadie, thank you for taking care of my boy. I'll be taking him home in two months." Sadie is happy that Jackson's father has come for him. With tears of joy in her eyes, she looks at Rev. Carolina and says, "Sir, I do the best that I can in taking care of your boy. He's like family to me. He's all that I've got, but I'm glad that you found your way to him. He has dreadfully missed you and the family."

CHAPTER 5

MT. MARIAH BAPTIST CHURCH

THREE YEARS LATER.

IT'S 1860. GRAND CANE, LOUISIANA. CAROLINA AND PATSY FULLER'S HOUSE IS ON TEN ACRES WITH HUGE CROPS OF COTTON, CORN, FRUIT TREES, SUGAR CANES, COWS, HORSES, ETC. JACKSON HAS BEEN HOME FOR THREE YEARS, AND HE'S TEN YEARS OLD. REV. CAROLINA STANDS IN THE FRONT YARD TALKING TO SEVERAL CHRISTIAN MEN WHO HELPED HIM ORGANIZE AND BUILD THE FIRST BLACK CHURCH IN DESOTO PARISH. IT'S CALLED "MT. MARIAH BAPTIST CHURCH."

Rev. Carolina is happy and has no complaints. Jackson is home, and there will be no more preaching under the "Brush Arbor." He's standing in front of his house speaking to the men who helped him build the church, "Brothers, tomorrow will be an exciting day. It will be the first day of worship in our new church. Be prepared to have a good time showing the Lord how grateful we are. It's God's will that churches be built in all black communities, and I'll see to it being done."

Patsy is inside finishing the new suit that she made for him to wear when he preaches his first sermon tomorrow morning. Jackson and the other children are busy with their chores. Jesse is too young to do anything; so, he stays close to his ma and his new sister, Irene.

10:00 A.M. SUNDAY. KINGSTON, LOUSIANA. MT. MARIAH BAPTIST CHURCH FIRST WORSHIP SERVICE.

Rev. Carolina is sitting in the pulpit wearing his new white suit with a black shirt and white tie. He's watching people enter the church while the musicians skillfully play some good toe-tapping music. His family is sitting on the front pew. Jackson is there with a smile on his face as he reminisces about the vision he had about the church long before it was built.

All the people are excited about worshiping inside the new church building. They're dressed in their best. Rev. Carolina is happily tapping his feet and moving his head from side to side to the rhythm of the music. He stands and walks up to the podium. Smiling, he looks out among the congregation and at his family. While the musicians are still playing their instruments, he closes his eyes, lifts his hands up towards heaven, and begins to sing.

1852 - 1919

"God has smiled on me
He has set me free
God has smiled on me
He has been so good to me.
When I was bound in chains
He sent the freedom train
I know that God has smiled on me
He's been good to me
Amazing grace how sweet the sound
He saved a wretch like me
God has smiled on me
He has set me free"

He stops singing and looks at the musicians, "Give me some African praise music. My father, Christopher Columbus, came from Africa in chains. He taught me a praise dance, and I'm going to do that dance for the Lord this morning. Y'all, don't let the whites make you forget who you are and where you came from. You don't have to look or act like them. God created us with our own beautiful characteristics. You must be proud to be African. God made us after his own image."

Rev. Carolina begins dancing the African praise dance. Some of the congregation rock in their seats and others jump up from their seats to dance. Finally, Rev. Carolina stops dancing, "Let the church say "Hallelujah, we are blessed. I'm here to tell you that God is a right now God – a present help in times of trouble. He has set us free to worship

1852 - 1919

him and to have a better life. With God on our side –
who can be against us? He's a bridge over troubled
waters. He broke away the chains of slavery and
gave us our own land. He's blessing us in many
ways. More blessings are coming – Jesus is going to
fix everything. Thank you, Jesus."

CHAPTER 6

JACKSON MEETS HIS SOUL MATE

JACKSON IS AGE 15. HE'S ATTENDING SCHOOL WITH TEN OTHER STUDENTS. THE TEACHERS ARE HUSBAND AND WIFE, MR. AND MRS. BROWN. MR. BROWN IS WRITING MATH QUESTIONS ON THE BLACK BOARD.

He finishes writing the questions, and looks at the students. Focusing on Jackson, who has his head down writing, he asks, "Jackson! What is the answer to $25 \div 850$?" Jackson looks at Mr. Brown and at the math question he's pointing towards. Without thinking he answers, "Sir, it's 34." Mr. Brown smiles because he isn't surprised that Jackson knew the answer. "Excellent." Next, Mr. Brown asks Jackson, "Multiply 34 x 78. What is the answer?" Again, Jackson immediately knows the answer and says, "Sir, it's 2,652." More impressed than before, Mr. Brown responds, "Excellent! Excellent! Jackson, you definitely have a gift for numbers."

Harriet, a pretty girl three years younger than Jackson, is sitting across from him. She's been admiring him for months and day dreams about him quite often. She passes a note to him and looks away quickly. Jackson takes the note and reads it; then, looks at her and smiles. He's a little shy and wants

43

to get to know Harriett but doesn't know how to go about it. He's thinks to himself, "She just made the first move by giving me the note. Maybe I can walk her home after school?"

After class, Jackson walks out of the building and sees Harriett talking to another girl. Cautiously, he walks over to her. She says goodbye to her friend and looks at Jackson with the most beautiful smile he's ever seen. Nervously, he begins to speak, "Hi Harriett! Thanks for the compliment in the note - it's real nice what you said. Would it be alright if I walk you home?" Harriett shyly looks down and says, "I would like that. Jackson! Do you study a lot? You know all of the answers no matter what the teacher asks." Jackson makes a gesture to take her books and replies, "Ah, yeah, I like to study. I guess I'm curious about a lot of things. Mostly, I study the Bible. When I study the Bible, I feel like God is talking to me." Harriett is surprised to hear that he likes reading the Bible and eagerly responds, "The Bible? I like studying the Bible too, but I get confused sometimes. Maybe we can study it together, and then I might understand it better." Jackson isn't quite as nervous anymore and replies, "Sure, we can do that." Harriett is a lot less shy too as she looks at Jackson and says, "You know, I think you are very special." Surprised at what she just said, he stands still, and looking at her says, "I'm glad you think that I'm special because I know you are special, and I knew it the first time I saw you.

44

Can I come visit you sometime?" Harriett very happily says, "Yes, I would like that. Well, here we are - home at last. Thank you, Jackson, for walking me home. Will I see you at church Sunday?" Jackson gives Harriett her books and promises, "I'll be there. See you then!"

IT'S EARLY AFTERNOON IN WOODED AREA WHERE THERE'S A BEAUTIFUL POND THAT'S SURROUNDED BY WILD FLOWERS AND GREEN GRASS.

Jackson is 19 years old, and Harriett is 16. They've been friends for four years and are very much in love. They're having a picnic in the woods near a pond where Harriett has a picnic basket packed with delicious food. She and Jackson are sitting on the blanket watching the movement of the water. Jackson asks her a question with a serious tone in his voice, "Harriett, we've been seeing each other for quite some time. Do you love me enough to become my wife?" Harriett takes his hand and assures him, "Yes, of course I do. I've been praying that you would ask me to marry you. You are asking me to marry you right?" He leans towards her and kisses her gently on her lips and asks, "Do you think your ma and pa will give us their blessings when I ask them for your hand in marriage?" Harriett is anxious for Jackson to properly propose and teasingly reproaches him, "I think they'll be just as happy as I'll be when you actually ask me to marry you."

Jackson reaches into his pocket for a beautiful diamond ring, and romantically gets on his knees. He places it on her finger and says, "Harriett! The first moment I first saw you, I thought you were the most beautiful girl I had ever seen. I knew then that one day I would want to marry you. Will you be my wife?" Harriett, getting on her knees and trying to look at the ring at the same time, throws her arms around Jackson's neck and begins kissing him all over his face. In between kisses she answers, "Yes, I'll marry you. It took you long enough to ask. Yes! Yes! I'll be your wife."

SIX MONTHS LATER

1:00 P.M. – MT. MARIAH CHURCH – JACKSON AND HARRIETT'S WEDDING.

Rev. Carolina marries Jackson and Harriett in front of a full congregation at Mt. Mariah Baptist Church. After they take their vows, they jump the broom and rush out of the church. People are throwing rice on them as they get into their wagon to go on their honeymoon.

ONE YEAR LATER

Rev. Carolina is having breakfast as Patsy sits across from him at the table drinking a cup of coffee and begins talking, "Carolina, I guess we can expect some grandchildren from Jackson and Harriett in the future. They've moved into their new home. He and his brothers did a fine job building the house; Stuart made some beautiful furniture for them; and, Dilsie and I made some mighty fine curtains, quilts and bed spreads. Giving them three acres of land is a good start; they're well on their way." Rev. Carolina stops eating and seriously responds, "You know, honey, all of our children are real smart. Jackson? I thank God for giving us a son like him. He's different than the others. He has a true connection with God, and I see him becoming someone powerful. Not many will be able to follow in his footsteps. I believe he's going to have whatever he wants in this life."

CHAPTER 7

REV. CAROLINA FULLER'S DEATH

Sixteen Years Later

Rev. Carolina Fuller died from a massive heart attack at the age of 71 on August 26, 1886 leaving his wife Patsy – age 68, four sons, and three daughters. He achieved his goals building churches throughout black communities in DeSoto Parish, Louisiana. He built two churches after building Mt. Mariah Baptist Church; New Bethlehem Baptist Church and Antioch Baptist Church. He saved many lost souls preaching the gospel and baptizing thousands. He was the Pastor of Mt. Mariah for 26 years.

Rev. Carolina Fuller's Funeral

**10:00 A.M. KINGSTON, LOUISIANA.
MT. MARIAH BAPTIST CHURCH AND CEMETERY.**

PEOPLE ARE IN ROUTE TO THE CHURCH; THEY ARE IN WAGONS, ON HORSES, AND MANY ARE WALKING LONG DISTANCES TO THE FUNNERAL. NOT EVERYONE IS ABLE TO ENTER THE CHURCH; SOME ARE STANDING IN THE CHURCH YARD.

1852 - 1919

The church bell is ringing as the wagon, carrying Rev. Carolina's body, enters Mt. Mariah's Church yard heading towards the front entrance of the church. The pallbearers are his four sons: Aaron, Jackson, Jesse and Stuart and two grandsons, Charlie and John. They're on horses following the wagon.

They remove the casket from the wagon and carry it into the church. The service lasts for more than three hours; and, there are more than 800 people attending. After the funeral service, the pallbearers carry the oak wood casket, made by Stuart, to the cemetery behind the church for burial. Dudley has his arms around his grandma Patsy and his ma, Harriett as they walk behind the casket. Dilsie, Gracie and Irene follow with their husbands at their sides, and a large crowd of people are not too far behind.

Rev. Huckabee officiates. He's the pastor of Antioch Baptist Church, the third church built by Rev. Carolina Fuller. He's known for becoming very theatrical without realizing it. Rev. Carolina's casket is placed on the ground near the grave. When all the people settle into their places, Rev. Huckabee begins, "We are gathered here this morning. (**He pauses and wipes his eyes with a handkerchief.**) Ah, to bury our beloved brother, Rev. Carolina Fuller. He was not only a father and husband; he was our God-Sent-Leader. A true man sent to us by God Almighty. (**He's moving his head from side to side**

and lifting his feet as though he's ready to march. When he realizes what he's doing, he grunts and is embarrassed.) Ah, I said, God Almighty – and all power is in his hands. God is a divine deliverer and he's a warrior. He'll fight your battles. (**Again, realizing what he's doing, he stops and coughs.**). Ah, Rev. Fuller was truly inspired and motivated by visions from God. He never let slavery hinder his life, and we can't let it hinder ours. Let me hear an Amen. I said, Let me hear an Amen. (**The people say Amen.**) That's what I'm talking about. Now, Rev. Fuller gave hope to all of us. He changed all of our lives. Bow your heads. Oh Lord, we send our brother Fuller home to you today, and we thank you for sending the Reverend into our lives. Watch over all of us and lead us onward. Amen."

Everyone leaves the cemetery except Jackson. Once alone with his pa, he kneels down by the casket to have his last conversation with him. He affectionately begins, "Pa, we've had a long journey together – from slavery to freedom. I'm going to miss you. I know I'm going see you again. God gave me another vision. He showed me establishing schools, becoming a Bishop, and owning lots of rich land. I promise you pa, I'm going to make you proud. At that very moment, a beautiful white dove appears and rests on Carolina's Casket. Jackson stands and stares at the dove. He smiles and walks away.

1852 - 1919

JACKSON'S WIFE, HARRIETT AND THEIR EIGHT SONS AND DAUGHTER (JOHN, CHARLIE, DUDLEY, CAROLINA, PRIMUS, JESSE, ROCHELLE, ERNEST, AND ALICE) ARE WAITING IN THE CHURCH YARD. THE YOUNGER CHILDREN ARE SITTING IN THE WAGON. JOHN, CHARLIE, AND DUDLEY ARE ON BEAUTIFUL HORSES WAITING TO FOLLOW THEIR FAMILY HOME.

Jackson walks from the cemetery towards Harriett and the children who wait in the wagon. He looks at his handsome sons, John, Charlie and Dudley who wait silently on their horses and says, "Sons, follow me back to the house." They answer in turn, "Yes sir, My Pappy." All of Jackson's children call him My Pappy. He quietly gets into the wagon and drives his family home without saying a word.

They ride down a dirt road in a heavily dense area of trees to a big beautiful two-story white house. It looks almost like the plantation house in South Carolina. The house is surrounded with flowering trees. It's sitting on approximately 25 acres with fields of cotton, sugar cane, vegetables, fruit trees, cows, horses and a big barn. There are men and women working the crops. Before Jackson can park the wagon in front of the house, the three boys race by the wagon as though they are being chased and head toward the barn.

51

Harriett finally breaks the silence, "Well, this has been a long difficult day. Children! I want all of you to go change your clothes and do your chores while I get dinner ready." The children answer, "Okay ma." They quickly get out of the wagon and run into the house. Jackson reaches for Harriett's hand before she can get out of the wagon. Looking at her tenderly he says, "Harriett, I love you. You know, this is the saddest day I've known. When I was sold away from my family at age five, I thought that was the worst day of my life. Losing pa is worst. It doesn't seem real. Baby, I feel a pain in my chest that I can't make go away."

Passionately, Harriett pulls Jackson towards her. She hugs him and offers these words of comfort, "Honey, listen to me. Pa Carolina is with the Lord, a much better place than here. We've got to be strong for ma Patsy. She was with pa through it all and for a long time. We all loved him, and we all are going to miss him. God has always been with you, and he's with you now. Everything is going to get better. I believe that pa has not gone far away. I believe he'll come to you in your dreams, and he'll live on in your heart." She kisses him, gets out of the wagon, and goes into the house.

The interior of the house is extravagantly beautiful. The window coverings are elaborate, the floors are shiny hardwood, and the furniture is covered with a colorful expensive embroider fabric. Harriett walks up the stairs and removes her hat. The children are upstairs playing and making lots of noise. She yells, "Stop playing and change your clothes. All of you have work to do before dinner time. The cows and horses need feeding, not to mention the chickens."

Jackson drives the wagon inside the barn to find Tyrone, one of his workers, there removing the saddles off the Clydesdale horses that Charlie, Dudley and John had just returned. Tyrone stops and goes towards Jackson to help with the wagon. "Good afternoon, sir. Sorry about your pa. Rev. Carolina was a good man."

Jackson gets down from the wagon, looks at Tyrone and politely responds, "Thank you, Tyrone. Pa is with God. He's gone to a better place." He walks towards his favorite horse, one that no one else can ride, a brown and blonde Clydesdale. He gets on it and rides out of the barn heading towards his crops to see how the workers are doing. With tears running down his face, he's remembering being with his father the morning that Master Wade came to take him to the auction. Suddenly, he stops riding, looks up towards heaven and yells, "My God, help me! Please take this pain away." At that very moment, Rev. Carolina's face appears up in the clouds. He's looking down at him smiling. It disappears as quickly as it appeared. Jackson has never experienced anything like this before. Seeing his pa's face smiling at him made the pain leave. Then, he knew then that his pa was alright. A comforting smile appears on his face; he turns and rides back to the house."

Rev. Carolina Fuller's Grave

**Mt. Mariah's Cemetery
located behind the church**

CHAPTER 8

A CHANGE IS COMING

SOUTH CAROLINA – JOSHUA'S FARM HAS BURNED DOWN. HE'S PACKING HIS WAGON TO MOVE TO KINGSTON, LOUISIANA TO FIND HIS FRIEND, REV. CAROLINA.

Joshua's wife has died, and his farm has been destroyed by fire. He and his neighbor are packing the wagon. Joshua is moving to Louisiana to find his best friend, Rev. Carolina. His neighbor is lifting a trunk into the wagon and asks, "Joshua, when was the last time you heard from Rev. Carolina?" Joshua is not aware that he has died and answers, "About five years ago. He's doing well and has built a church called Mt. Mariah. I figure, if I find the church, then I'll find Carolina. Since my wife has gone to be with the Lord, I don't have a reason to stay in South Carolina."

ONE YEAR LATER – 1887

Jackson is now 35 years old, and he and Harriett have nine children. It's an early Saturday evening and he's sitting around the table with the younger children teaching them math and having them read out loud. The table is covered with paper, pencils and books. Sitting around the table are: Jesse - age

14, Rochelle - age 13, Carolina – age 12, Ernest - age 11, Alice - age 8 and Dilsie is age 5. Jackson enjoys studying with his children, and he's determined that they all become educated.

Harriett is sitting nearby at the sewing machine. She's finishing a new suit for Jackson to wear the next morning when he preaches his first sermon at Mt. Mariah. He has been pastor for the past ten years at Bethlehem Baptist, the second church built by his father. Mt. Mariah Baptist Church has recently appointed him to become their new pastor. Harriett sits, holding up the jacket and admiring her work. She proudly says, "Honey, you're going to look mighty fine in this suit tomorrow morning." Jackson stops studying with the children and responds, "Baby, I like what I see. You're doing a mighty fine job making that suit." Harriett with a proud look on her face admiring the suit says, "I'll be finished in a few minutes. It's time for the children to go to bed. We've got to get up early for church in the morning." Jackson agrees, "Okay, enough studying for tonight. All of you are smart, but next week, I expect for you to be smarter. Go upstairs and get ready for bed. Alice! Help Dilsie get ready for bed."

After clearing the table of papers and books, Harriett and Jackson go upstairs to their bedroom. Harriett props up on some pillows while waiting for Jackson. She watches him stand in front of the mirror holding his new suit in admiration. Laughing as he dances in his long johns, he blurts out, "Wife, you sure do know how to make your man look good. This is a mighty fine suit." She responds, "Honey, I'm glad you like it. You're going to be the handsomest man at church. Now, come to bed and warm me up. My feet are cold." Jackson hangs his new suit in the closet and playfully says, "You don't have to ask me twice. I'm coming." He gets into bed and pulls Harriett close to him and begins kissing her. Just as the mood becomes intimate, Dilsie abruptly opens their bedroom door. Running into the room, she jumps on the bed and yells, "My Pappy, I'm afraid of the boogeyman." She gets underneath the covers between them and falls asleep soon after her head touches the pillow.

THE NEXT MORNING - SUNDAY

It's June 1, 1887. Today is Rev. Jackson Fuller's first day as pastor of Mt. Mariah Baptist Church. The church is crowded with people and the musicians are playing. Jackson feels very connected to his pa and to God as he sits in the pulpit watching the congregation. Harriett and the children are sitting on the front pew; everyone else is seated and waiting for Rev. Jackson to approach the podium. The musicians stop playing their worship music. Jackson stands and walks up to the podium. He looks very handsome wearing his new black and grey pin striped three piece suit accessorized with a black shirt, grey tie and black shoes.

1852 - 1919

"Good morning saints. I'm going to begin with scriptures. **II Samuel 6:14 'And David danced before the Lord with all his might', and Psalms 30:11 'Thou hath turned for me my mourning into dancing: thou hast put off my sackcloth, and girded me with gladness.'**

"I thought it was going to be very difficult for me to stand here this morning as your pastor without becoming emotional over the loss of my pa. Rev. Carolina Fuller preached here at Mt. Mariah for 26 years. To my surprise, my heart is glad this morning. I'm proud that you all appointed me to take his place as your pastor."

"According to the scriptures that I read, David danced before the lord when he became King. I feel like David this morning. I'm going to dance a praise dance that my pa danced for God when he learned that the time had come for him to escape from slavery. This praise dance is from the mother land, Africa. My grandfather, Christopher Columbus, came to America bound in chains from Africa. He taught the dance to my pa, and pa taught it to me. Now, I'm going to show you. It is good to praise God with a dance. People, no matter what, we must never forget that we are Africans; and that God gave us a praise dance.

Musicians, play me some praise music."

In the pulpit, Jackson begins praising God with an African praise dance. At first, the congregation is stunned. Slowly, some of them feel the spirit and jump to their feet with a dance. Jackson finishes his dance. He wipes the perspiration from his face with a handkerchief and begins to speak.

"When I stand here this morning, I visualize my pa, Rev. Carolina Fuller, standing right here beside me with a smile on his face. As the Lord leads me with his visions and with his word, I'll lead you. Amen? We all were in chains together, and together we sojourned to freedom. God is blessing us. We are a spiritual and wise creation of God. As long as we keep him first, he'll fight our battles in this foreign land called America. With God on our side, who can be against us? We must continue to pray together, to walk together, and love one another in order to survive among those who hate us because of the color of our skin. Our people are still being persecuted by most of the whites. Our houses are being burned to the ground, and we are still being hung from trees and murdered in ruthless ways. God is watching. He sits high, but his eyes are looking low. We must trust him for everything. He is a present help in times of trouble." When he finishes speaking, he begins to sing,

"Don't let this world mislead you
Don't you ever go astray
Trust in God's Word and believe it

It will never pass away
See Him in his glory
Riding on the clouds of joy
Greeting us with open arms
And peace forever more
I know that everything is going to be alright."

After church service, Jackson stands at the front door talking and shaking hands with the congregation as they leave.

TEN YEARS LATER – 1897

Jackson is age 45. His business endeavors are becoming phenomenal. He and Harriett have purchased more than 860 acres of land that's enriched with minerals and timber. Their ranch is bringing in huge profits from crops of cotton, fruit orchards, cattle and hogs, etc. And, it is known for giving away food to many people who are in need. There are only five children living at home with Jackson and Harriett: Alice, Dilsie, Gracie, Mimie and Clifton. The other eight are living in their own homes on land given to them by their parents. Each child was given 40 acres of land and $60 in gold when they moved away from home.

CHAPTER 9

WHITE MAN LIVING ON DUDLEY'S LAND

GRAND CANE, LOUISIANA. THERE IS A SMALL CABIN IN THE MIDDLE OF THE WOODS FAR AWAY FROM EVERYONE.

It's mid-afternoon and Dudley is on his land riding his horse. He decides to go far into the woods for the first time to see if there are any ponds where he might go fishing. After riding several hours, he notices smoke going straight up in the air. Following the direction of the smoke, he eventually sees a small cabin with smoke coming out of the chimney. There's an old white man sitting on the porch. As Dudley gets closer, the old man reaches for a rifle and points it at him.

Dudley rides slowly towards the cabin, and when he gets fifty feet from it, the old man yells, "Don't come any closer. What are you doing here?" Dudley stops and challenges the old man, "Don't shoot old man. I believe I should be asking you that question. This is my land, and if I remember right, I never invited you to set up house here." The old man answers, "I've lived here for years without any disturbances. It never occurred to me anybody would have any claim to land way out here. Do you have papers to prove that you own this land?" Dudley, shifting uneasily on his horse answers, "Are you questioning me because I'm a nigger to you? You think a nigger don't own land here in Louisiana? Well, you better think again." The old man, still pointing his rifle at Dudley quickly answers, "No sir, I don't judge a man by the color of his skin. I don't mean to give you a bad time. I guess I find it hard to believe after living here all these years, that you're here today claiming this property. I apologize if I've offended you." Dudley can see that the old man is genuinely upset and answers reassuringly, "Sir, do you mind if I sit and talk to you?" The old man lowers his rifle, lays it near his chair, then looks at Dudley and calmly says, "I guess it would be the right thing to do since you say you own this land." Dudley gets off his horse; he goes and sits in the other chair and asks, "What is your name? Why are you way out here in the middle of no man's land?" The old man plainly answers, "My name is Joshua McBride. After my property was destroyed from the war and my wife died, I left and headed to Louisiana to find my friend. Ten years ago, on my way from Columbia, South Carolina, I had an accident and injured my head. I lost my memory and couldn't remember anything for a long time. Finally, some of my memory started coming back, but I couldn't remember my friend's name. I could only remember that he was in Kingston, Louisiana somewhere. Without a name, there is no way for me to find him. So, I reckoned that I would find me a spot in the middle of nowhere and set up house as you say."

Dudley is thinking to himself that since Joshua is white, most likely his friend is white. He responds, "Well, what you just told me is a sad story. We need to talk more and come up with a solution about you living here. It will be dark in a little while, so I need to head back. Do you think you can come to my house on Sunday afternoon around 3:00 p.m. so we can talk? I live around 10 miles west of here. Just keep straight up the path and you'll see a big brown house. Be prepared to have dinner with my family. I sure hope you won't feel uncomfortable eating with black folks." Joshua, looking a bit relaxed, answers, "Like I said before, I don't judge a man by the color of his skin. God created us all. It is mighty fine of you not to kick me off your land right now and to invite me to your house. You can count on me being there. What is your last name, sir?" Dudley smiles, "Just call me Dudley."

The next morning, Dudley is on his way to meet his brother, Charlie, to go to the market in Mansfield to deliver sugar canes from the family ranch. On his way, he stops by his pa's. Jackson is standing on his porch stretching his arms when Dudley rides into the yard. He greets him, "Good morning, son! I'm surprised to see you. I thought you and Charlie had work to do. What's going on with the sugar canes? Aren't you taking them to the market today?" Dudley doesn't get off his horse and answers, "I'm on my way to meet Charlie. I came by to tell you that yesterday while riding in the woods, I discovered an old white man living on my land. After talking to him, I felt sorry for him. I invited him to come by the house Sunday afternoon at 3:00 to talk about the situation. I want to know if you would be there when he comes." Jackson looks at Dudley with squinted eyes as though he's trying to figure out who is the stranger, and finally asks, "What do you plan to do about this man? What is his name and where did he come from? Dudley watches his pa's face intently as Jackson continues to squint his eyes, and he answers, "He said his name is Joshua McBride and that he came from South Carolina to Louisiana to find his friend." Hearing the name Joshua and South Carolina, Jackson sits in a chair and rubs his mustache. He speculates, "Son, that name sounds familiar. I reckon I should meet this man. I'll be there after church." Jackson repeats the name over and over again until a flash of recognition spreads over his face, "Joshua...Joshua...No! Can it be Joshua, pa's friend?"

Sunday afternoon after church, Jackson goes directly to Dudley's house to meet Joshua. He's curious as to whether Joshua is his pa's best friend. He's arrives a little early. Dudley is glad to see him. Dudley is a little anxious about the old white man coming to his home, and he's eager to find out if he's his grandpa's friend.

Jackson and Dudley settle down in the living room, and Jackson begins, "Son, I've been thinking about this man, Joshua. If I'm right, it's a miracle. When pa was on the plantation in South Carolina, he had a white friend that he grew up with named Joshua. Joshua taught pa how to read from the Bible and how to swim. When pa started preaching to the slaves far out in the woods under a "Brush Arbor," Joshua was there with his rifle and dog standing guard against white intruders. Good Lord! Joshua even helped the family and all of Master Wade's slaves escape to Louisiana. Surely, this cannot be the same man."

It's a little before 3:00 p.m., and Joshua drives his wagon into Dudley's yard. He sits for a while and looks up towards the sky and whispers a little prayer to God, "Lord, I don't know what to expect when I go into Mr. Dudley's house. I trust in you that everything is going to be alright. I don't have anywhere to go if he asks me to get off of his land." He gets down from the wagon and slowly walks up on the porch and knocks. Dudley quickly gets up and opens the front door greeting him, "Hello Joshua, I'm glad you made it. Come on in." Joshua enters and graciously says, "Thank you." He looks at Jackson who is standing and looking at him with his mouth open as though he sees a ghost. Joshua introduces himself, "Hello, sir. My name is Joshua McBride." Jackson walks hurriedly towards Joshua and yells, "I don't believe my eyes. My Lord, it is you. Joshua McBride!" Joshua looks at Jackson with a puzzled look on his face, and pauses, "I don't understand. You know me?" Jackson, extending his hand to shake Joshua's responds, "I'm Jackson, Carolina's boy from the plantation in South Carolina."

Joshua shakes Jackson's hand. Staring at him as though he's trying to remember, responds as though he is in shock, "This cannot be. I remember. Carolina! You're Jackon?" He immediately hugs him. Holding back tears, he says, "I remember." Letting go of Jackson, Joshua asks, "Where is Carolina? Dudley! You're Carolina's grandson? Thank God, I have found Carolina. Where is he?" Tears of joy are running down his face. Feeling sorry for Joshua, Jackson solemnly says, "Pa died 10 years ago, and I still miss him." Jackson takes Joshua's arm and leads him to a chair. Dudley rushes into the kitchen and returns with a glass of water for Joshua. When Joshua stops crying, he looks away from both Dudley and Jackson and finally speaks, "Carolina is gone. He was my best friend, and I've come so far to find him. It had to be God who led me to your land. I'm sitting here with my best friend's family. This is a miracle."

Later, Dudley, Jackson and Joshua are sitting around the dinner table eating. Dudley's wife, Henry Lee, has cooked corn bread, mustard greens, potato salad, fried chicken and corn on the cob with peach cobbler for dessert. She's gone with the children to visit her ma and pa so that the men could talk without disturbance from the children. Joshua is eating none stop as though he hasn't had a meal in days. Jackson stops eating and says, "Joshua, I'm glad God has led you to us. I want you to know that you don't have to worry about anything. You took care of my pa and saw to it that my family got away from Master Wade. I've been blessed with more than enough. I want to do something special for you. You have shown my family much love, and to me you are family. Your worries are over. Where you're living is too far away from everyone. I don't want you to live away from the family. If it's okay with you, I would like to give you some land closer to the family and build you a new house. This way I can make sure you're cared for properly. How does that sound?" Joshua, teary eyed, looks at Dudley and then he looks at Jackson and says, "It sounds like the music to my ears. The best music I've ever heard. Bless you Jackson, bless you." Joshua looks up towards the ceiling and gives praise, "Thank you God!" Dudley hasn't been able to touch his food very much because of the excitement. He's been busy listening and looking at his My Pappy and Joshua. Finally, he speaks, "Well, the situation is settled. Welcome to the family, Joshua."

Jackson has left Dudley and Joshua and decides to stop by his son, Carolina's house. He named Carolina after his pa. As he rides his Clydesdale horse towards Carolina's house, he sees him outside raking leaves. Carolina stops working and greets his Pa, "My Pappy, what brings you by today?" Jackson doesn't intend to stay long, so he stays on his horse and replies, "I didn't see you in church this morning, and I wanted to make sure you didn't get into any trouble last night. Were you out late at that dance shack place?" Jackson can tell he's recovering from bootleg liquor. "I hope not. That place is trouble." Carolina respects his pa and knows that he often times knows things without anybody telling him. He sits in a chair underneath the tree and looks at Jackson. "No, My Pappy, I stayed home. Charlie, John, Jesse and Primus came over and we sat around and played dominos most of the night. I won't miss church next Sunday."

Jesse is inside the house and hears Jackson talking. He has a terrible hangover from drinking too much liquor last night. He walks out on the porch. "Morning My Pappy, I guess you're surprised to see me here, huh! I stayed over because it was too late to go home alone in the dark. You know how those red necks are waiting to kill a black man riding alone." Jackson, surprised to see Jesse, looks at him with a raised eyebrow, and reprimands, "Good morning, Jesse. I need not ask you why you didn't come to church. Now, I've trained you boys that you've got to keep God first in your life. He'll protect you from evil, like those so-called red necks you're talking about." Jesse feels a little guilty about missing church and sheepishly looks at his pa and says, "Sir, you're right, and I won't miss another Sunday. My Pappy, I've been meaning to ask you. Do you think all of us boys can go hunting with you sometime this week? I know you're busy and all, but it sure would be nice, don't you think? Jackson smiles and looking at his boys, he answers, "Why not? I'll make the time. I want all eight of you boys to be at the house Friday at noon. Make sure this time your shot guns are cleaned. Yeah, it would be good to spend some time with my sons. I've got to go, and I'll see you Friday."

CHAPTER 10

JACKSON'S SONS

Jackson and Harriett are in their bedroom getting ready for bed. Harriett is sitting at the dresser in front of the mirror brushing her long black hair. Jackson, wearing long johns, is sitting on the side of the bed watching her. He has a lot on his mind after seeing Carolina and Jesse earlier in the day, and says, "Harriett, I'm worried about Carolina and Jesse. I hear they spend a lot of time around that Juke Joint called 'The CrossRoads Cafe'. I stopped by Carolina's house before coming home, and I could smell the bootleg liquor coming from his pores. Jesse was there, and came out on the porch looking like he had been drugged. He asked if I would go hunting with all of the boys. I agreed. Maybe I'll be able to talk to them about keeping God first in their lives. I'm not taking Clifton hunting until he becomes a bit older. Our sons know that most of the colored folks around here don't like the Fullers because we've been blessed with wealth. Jealousy is a monster from hell. They've got to be careful of where they go and how much they drink. I see bad trouble for Carolina and Jesse. God help them."

Harriett stops brushing her hair and goes over to the bed. Pulling back the covers, she takes Jackson by the arm and urges, "Honey, come to bed and get some rest. We just have to keep praying for God to take care of our children. That's all we can do. We taught them to fear the Lord, and we have to believe that God will protect them from being harmed by those who hate us."

Jackson gets into bed, and adds, "Oh, I almost forgot. Today at Dudley's, I met the old white man who's living on his land. He's Joshua McBride, pa's friend from South Carolina. He moved to Louisiana to find pa. During his travels, he had a head injury and lost his memory. He couldn't remember pa. He only knew to come to this area. Can you believe it? God has sent him to us ten years after pa has been gone."

It's Friday, almost noon, and it's time to go hunting. Jackson's sons are waiting in the back yard for their My Pappy to come out of the house. Jackson comes out on the back porch carrying his rifle and smiling. He greets them, "Good morning, or is it noon? I see y'all are ready to go hunting. Are your rifles cleaned?" Dudley looks at his brothers, and holding up his rifle, he says, "I always keep my rifle clean. I don't know about Rochelle. I don't think he knows how to clean his riffle." Rochelle laughs and responds, "You want to bet some money on it? It's as clean as a whistle." Jackson is ready to head for the woods, as the other boys laugh and joke around and he says, "Let's go and see what we can shoot today." He walks towards the woods with his eight

1852 - 1919

sons. Looking back at Harriett and Clifton standing on the porch, he hollers, "Harriett, I'm going to bring you back a wild turkey." Clifton, stands next to his ma, watching them disappear into the woods. He's sad because he wants to go with them, and complains, "Ma, how much longer do I have to wait before I can go hunting?" She puts her arm around his shoulders, and assures him, "Son, when you get a little older. Don't you like staying here to protect me while all the men folks are away?"

1852 - 1919

CHAPTER 11

DESOTO PARISH FIRST BLACK SCHOOLS

Jackson Fuller has become Bishop, a Moderator Chairman of the Northwest Association No. 2 District. This covers territory throughout DeSoto Parish. He presides over more than 30 churches with credit, having succeeded himself many times. He held and now holds some of the highest positions as a shepherd of some of the state's best churches, and he's known as one of the most esteemed Christian leaders.

Seeing the necessity to educate black children, he is spearheading and establishing accredited schools at every black church throughout DeSoto Parish. He and his partner, Mr. Haynes, are interviewing and hiring the best educators they can find to teach at the schools.

Jackson is sitting in his office at Mt. Mariah Baptist Church with his business partner, Mr. Haynes and the newly hired teacher, Mr. Moore. Jackson and Mr. Haynes have recently gotten the state of Louisiana's Board of Education to certify accreditation of Mt. Mariah's new school. Jackson hands Mr. Moore the papers, "Here are the certification papers from the Louisiana State Board of Education stating that Mt. Mariah's school is fully accredited. Mr. Haynes and I have made the necessary preparations for you and your wife to relocate. Your new house is within walking distance. Also, we have set up an account for your monthly salary and for purchasing school supplies."

Mr. Moore is excited about being hired as the new teacher at Mt. Mariah's school. He had written a letter to Jackson inquiring about the position. He responds, "Rev. Jackson, I know how important this school is to you and Mr. Haynes. I'm much obliged that you hired me to be the teacher; I promise you that you will not regret your decision." Mr. Haynes extends his hand to the new teacher. "Welcome, Mr. Moore. We are glad to have you." They get up and go outside the church. Jackson says his goodbyes, gets into his car, and heads to the next meeting that's taking place at Antioch Baptist Church.

Arriving at Antioch Baptist Church, the third church that was built by his father, he goes inside where pastors are waiting to meet with him. "Good Afternoon Pastors! It's good seeing all of you." Jackson sits at the table with them. "I hope y'all have looked over the budgets and plans to establish state accredited schools at Antioch, Bethlehem, and all the other churches in our communities. As y'all know, it is necessary to educate all of our children. Having said that, I would like to hear your thoughts and any suggestions you may have regarding the budgets and plans. Let's start with the Bethlehem School.

1852 - 1919

The budgets and plans were discussed in depth and all pastors approved them. State accredited schools and colleges for black children are being established throughout the state of Louisiana. Jackson is being inundated with letters from black educators from all over the south inquiring about available teaching positions.

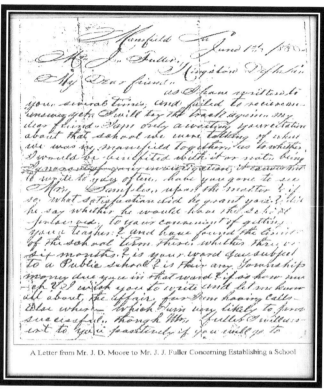

A Letter from Mr. J. D. Moore to Mr. J. J. Fuller Concerning Establishing a School

Mr. Moore wrote the above letter to Jackson in June 1880 inquiring about a teacher's position and the status of the school's establishment and state's accreditation.

Robert Y. Haynes, Sr.
(Former Slave)
Jackson's Business Partner

CHAPTER 12

THE CROSSROADS CAFÉ INCIDENT

MANSFIELD, LOUISIANA.

Carolina is headed to the CrossRoads Café in Mansfield in his new fancy car with his brothers, Dudley and Jesse. It's Saturday night around 10:00 p.m. The CrossRoads Café is a juke joint that serves bootleg liquor and has a blues band that plays good music. Almost every evening, wild men and women can be found here dancing and getting drunk. Carolina parks his car where there are only horses and wagons. Most blacks don't have cars because they can't afford them.

Looking at his brothers, Carolina asks, "Y'all have your pistols in case there's trouble?" Dudley gets out of the car and boasts, "Man, I'm always ready. You know that son-of-a–bitch Roscoe is going be waiting for you. Carolina, he hates you because of Annie Farris. His favorite saying is that one day he's going to kill you." Jesse is still in the car putting his pistol in his boot, "We can't get into any trouble tonight. My Pappy will kill us himself if we do. We've got to be cool and not get drunk. In the morning, the revival starts, and we promised My Pappy that we would be at church." Carolina walks towards the café and grimly says, "Okay, Jesse, we hear you loud and clear. Let's go inside and have some fun."

78

1852 - 1919

All three of them are dressed in black. Their shirts are half way unbutton and they're wearing wide cowboy hats. Entering the café, it's crowded and the band is playing a song called "Crossroads." They stand near the door looking for an available table to sit. Carolina leaves them and goes to a table where people are sitting. He bends down and whispers something in a man's ear and hands him money. The people get up from the table and leave. He beckons for his brothers to come. All eyes are on them; the ladies are admiring them, and the men are despising them. When Dudley and Jesse join Carolina at the table, Carolina says, "Man, when you've got money, you don't have to worry about where you're going to sit." Dudley is upset about what Carolina did, and says disapprovingly, "Carolina, man, you shouldn't have done that. Now, you've got the brothers in here hating on us. You know most of these guys hate us." Carolina, looking nonchalant says, "Man, it is - what it is."

Roscoe is drunk and dances his way over to the table where they're sitting. He slurs, "Carolina! Have you seen Annie lately? I hope not, for your sake, because she belongs to me." Carolina looks angrily at Roscoe and says, "Roscoe, get your drunk ass out of my face. You're dreaming if you think Annie will look at a poor ass fool like you."

Immediately, Jesse tries to prevent a fight and says, "Man, don't give Roscoe a reason to fight. You know he's crazy. Let it go and let's just have a good time. Roscoe, we don't want any trouble tonight. Man, let me buy you a drink." The mention of a free drink distracts Roscoe from Carolina, and he gladly accepts, "Jesse, you're alright. Come on and buy me a drink, man." Carolina watches Jesse almost having to carry Roscoe to the bar. He's so drunk, he can hardly walk. Carolina, disapprovingly, shakes his head and says, "I was about ready to hurt Roscoe. Dudley, look at that beautiful woman sitting over there staring at me. I'm going over there to see if I can get a little action." He gets up from the table and goes to where the lady is sitting. She eagerly makes room for him to join her.

Dudley is left alone at the table sitting with his back to the wall. He has a drink in one hand. With his other hand, he removes his pistol from his boot. He keeps the pistol in his hand underneath the table and watches both brothers to make sure none of their enemies try to hurt them. Carolina and the woman are dancing fancy steps on the dance floor. Jesse leaves Roscoe at the bar and goes to ask a lady to dance. They join Carolina and his lady friend on the dance floor. Normally, there's a fight at the café every night. Tonight, there is no trouble; everybody is having fun.

It's almost closing time, and the lights begin to flicker at the Café. Carolina, Dudley and Jesse decide to leave before everyone else. They don't want to be caught outside in the dark with the crowd. As they get close to the car, they notice that it has been damaged. The car's back lights and window are broken and the paint is scratched. Carolina becomes enraged and starts cursing, "That son-of-a-bitch, Roscoe, he's dead. I'm going to kill that bastard. Look at what he did to my car." Dudley attempts to get Carolina into the car, and quickly says, "Man, you don't know if Roscoe did this. It could have been any of those brothers inside the café." Jesse gets into the car, and replies, "Let's get out of here. Carolina, you've got to get this car fixed before My Pappy finds out what happened. We should have listened to him. He told us to stay away from this place. Let's go before something else bad happens."

They speed away from the parking lot. Shortly after leaving Mansfield city limits, they're driving down a rural road headed towards home when a police car turns on the siren and comes up behind them. Carolina nervously yells, "Oh! Hell no. The police are behind us. Y'all put your pistols on top of your heads underneath your hats. Make sure your hats are pulled down tight so the pistols don't move. This way if they search us, they won't find weapons. They probably won't ask us to take off our hats." Dudley takes off his hat and reaches for his pistol in his boot. "Man, how did you come up with this idea? Pistol on my head? Underneath my hat? It's brilliant. Carolina, let me do the talking. Your temper is too bad to deal with these red neck bastards. They may try to kill us out here on this dark road." Carolina pulls over to the side of the road and stops the car. He replies, "Dudley, do your thing. I won't say a word."

The policemen get out of their patrol car and walk slowly, carrying a pistol in one hand and a flashlight in the other. They shine the lights into the car and into Carolina's face; the first policeman rudely says, "Where do you niggers think you're going so early in the morning without back lights and a broken window? All of you get out of the car. What are your names? Show me some I.D. Whose car is this? What's a nigger doing driving a new car? The second policeman stands nearby shining his flashlight on them and aiming his pistol at Carolina's head. The look of hatred on his face is obvious that he would like to shoot them.

Carolina, Dudley and Jesse are standing outside the car facing the policemen. Dudley answers the first policeman, "Sir, to answer your questions, we're on our way home from The CrossRoads Café. Somebody broke the car window and lights while we were inside. This car belongs to my brother, Carolina, and he has the papers to prove it. Sir, we're Bishop Jackson Fuller's sons; we don't want any trouble with the law."

The first policeman angrily stares at them as though he wants to do harm, and says rudely, "I don't give a shit whose sons you are. Show me some I.D. I've heard all about you Fuller niggers. You are niggers no matter how much money you've got. As far as I'm concern, all of you goddamn niggers should still be in chains working the fields. Here you are driving a new car. Hell, I can't afford a new car." He looks at his partner and orders, "Jimmy, break the goddamn front window." The second policeman puts his gun in the holster and pulls out his police baton and breaks the front car window. Laughing, he returns and stands next to his partner. He attaches his baton to his belt and removes his gun and starts pointing it at them again.

The first policeman is chewing gum, smiling, and staring a Carolina while waving his gun in his face. He can tell that Carolina is becoming very angry, and he's trying to provoke him to do something to justify shooting them. Finally, he drawls, "I should take all three of you darkies back to town and show you what we do to niggers behind bars. I'm going to let y'all go this time, but if I see you driving again without lights or windows, I'm taking you in. Now, get your black asses out of here before I change my mind."

Carolina can hardly contain himself. Pretending that he's thankful, he bows his head and reaches for his hat while thanking the policeman. He wants to shoot both of them with the gun beneath his hat. Jesse knows what Carolina is doing and cleverly reaches for his arm to stop him.

As the policemen drive away, Carolina is so angry that Jesse has to drive them home. Jesse looks at Carolina, and exhales, "Man that was close. What were you thinking? The white folks around here will hang us from the tallest tree had you killed those policemen." Carolina has calmed down a little and says, "Y'all, I came very close to killing both of those red neck bastards. Thank you Jesse for keeping me from killing them." Dudley finally speaks, "I'm glad we made it out of that situation alive. The first policeman looked as though he wanted to get rid of all three of us. The second one was a flunky following orders. Jesse! Can't you drive faster? You're driving like an old lady." All three of them start laughing.

1852 - 1919

CHAPTER 13

THE CHURCH YARD SHOOTING

EARLY SUNDAY MORNING. OUTSIDE OF MT. MARIAH BAPTIST CHURCH.

Mt. Mariah's Baptist Church parking lot is filled with wagons, horses, a few carriages and the Fullers' cars. Music is coming from inside the church. Today is the first day of revival. Roscoe walks towards the church door carrying two armadillos in a cage, and he's going to let them loose inside to disrupt the congregation. He hopes the distraction will prevent the congregation from hearing the gun shot when he kills Carolina. Roscoe slightly opens the church door and the cage. The two armadillos run inside the church. Roscoe quietly closes the church door and runs back to the nearby trees. There, he waits for Carolina to arrive. He's been drinking and is talking to himself, "Those armadillos are going to get everybody upset. Nobody will be able to hear the gun when I shoot Carolina."

Inside the church, the armadillos run down the center aisle and into the pews. They're running fast in every direction. Screaming, all the ladies get up on the pews while the men try to catch the two frantic animals. Standing in the pulpit, Bishop Jackson yells, "Hurry and catch those armadillos."

Matilda is the church's nurse. She's wearing an all white nurse's uniform complete with: white dress, short cape, nurse's hat with a white dove feather standing straight up on the side of it. She's very theatrical as she hollers and runs to get away from the armadillos, "Somebody! Do something about those armadillos. Oh Sweet Jesus! One is coming my way." She runs to the pulpit and is holding on to Bishop Jackson. She pleads, "Lord Jesus help us; we're being attacked by armadillos." Bishop Jackson is trying to make her let go. He yells, "Nurse Matilda! Get a hold of yourself. Deacons! Ushers! Get something and catch those armadillos." He's continues to struggle with Nurse Matilda who won't let go of him.

Carolina and Jesse ride their horses into the church yard. While tying their horses to a pole, Carolina cautiously looks around and says, "Jesse, I've got a gut feeling that Roscoe is going to be here this morning. I've got my pistol in case that bastard wants some more of last night. If I don't shoot him today, it will be another day." Jesse begins looking around to see if Roscoe is there, and says, "He can't be that crazy to start trouble here at the church. If he's the one who jacked up your car, he's going try to get you before you get him. So, you're going to have to be very watchful." Carolina stares at the church and says, "Do you hear screaming coming from the church? Sound like something is wrong. The revival can't be that good." Jesse heads quickly towards the church, and urgently says, "Something is wrong. We better check it out."

As Carolina and Jesse rush toward the church, Roscoe runs out from the trees with a pistol in his hand, and yells out, "Carolina! It's time for you to meet your maker." He shoots Carolina in the head between his eyes. Before Carolina falls to the ground, he shoots Roscoe in the head.

Jesse screams, "Carolina!" He rushes over to Roscoe who is still standing and holding the pistol. He knocks him to the ground and starts beating him not realizing that Roscoe has been shot in the head. He yells, "You killed Carolina, and now I'm going to kill you."

The congregation hear the gun shots and forget about the armadillos. Immediately, they all run out of the church to see what has happened. To avoid the crowd hording at the church's front door, Jackson runs out the side door. He sees Carolina lying on the ground in a pool of blood beneath his head, and yells, "Carolina! My boy has been shot in the head." He looks and sees Jesse beating and kicking Roscoe who looks dead. Jackson shouts, "Primus! Dudley! Stop Jesse from killing that man. Charlie! Rochelle! Help me with Carolina. John! Drive the car over here. We've got to get Carolina to the Sanctuary. Where is Nurse Matilda?" He yells, "Nurse Matilda! Come help stop the bleeding. Ernest! Clifton! Take your ma and sisters home. They don't need to see this. Nurse Matilda! Where is she? Nurse Matilda!"

Nurse Matilda recovers from the excitement of the armadillos, and comes out of the church. When she hears the Bishop calling her, she rushes through the crowd to the sound of Jackson's voice. She's yelling, "Move out of the way, medical care is being called upon. Move out the way. I'm coming Bishop. Oh Lord, help me. I'm coming." Finally, she sees Carolina lying on the ground motionless and bleeding. Dramatically, she tosses her snow white cape to the ground to kneel on it. With her teeth, she rips the hem of her white dress to get fabric to cover and apply pressure to Carolina's head wound.

Jackson is on his knees holding Carolina's head. He cries out to God.

"Almighty God, my son is lying here in a pool of flowing blood. In the name of Jesus, I send your word to Carolina knowing that it will prosper where it is sent and will not return unto you void of power. In Ezekiel 16:6, you gave Ezekiel power to stop the bleeding, and now I ask that you give that power to me. Thank you, Jesus. Carolina! As I see you polluted in your own blood, I say unto you live. Yes, I say unto you live."

Nurse Matilda removes her hand from applying pressure to rip more clean fabric from her dress. She notices that the bleeding has stopped. "Bishop! Bishop! The bleeding has stopped! The bleeding has stopped! My God, the spirit of the Lord is here. The bleeding has stopped!" The people, standing around watching, begin whispering to one another. "The bleeding has stopped. God heard Bishop Fuller's prayer and answered."

Harriett struggles to get away from Ernest who is trying to get her into the car, and she screams, "Jackson, I need to go with you to the sanctuary. My boy has been shot, and I need to be with him." Alice, Gracie, Dilsie and Mimie struggle to get through the crowd to reach Carolina. They're crying and screaming Carolina's name; Alice screams as loudly as she can, "My Pappy is Carolina dead? Is Carolina dead?" Jackson is trying to take care of Carolina. Again, he yells, "Ernest! Clifton! Take your ma and sisters home. They can't do anything here and don't need to see Carolina like this."

Ernest is very upset, and while trying the get his sisters and ma into the car, he yells for Clifton to come and help him, "Where is Clifton? Clifton! Come help me get them into the Car." In the meantime, his sister's are still trying to get to Carolina. Finally, Clifton makes his way to Ernest and helps him get everyone inside the car. Crying and screaming, Harriett is practically pushed into the car as she asks, "Is Carolina dead? Is my baby dead?" Ernest reaches for his ma. He's hugging her and whispers, "Ma, you know My Pappy isn't going to let him die." Clifton drives away from the church as fast as he can to get them home so that he and Ernest can go to the sanctuary in Mansfield.

Jackson and Charlie lift unconscious Carolina into the back seat of the car, and Charlie gets in to hold his head. John drives away as fast as he can and heads to the Mansfield's Sanctuary. Nurse Matilda, covered in blood, watches them drive away. she starts praying aloud, "Sweet Jesus! I know your spirit is here. I saw how you stopped the flowing blood from Carolina's head. I'm asking you to please don't let him die. Amen."

CHAPTER 14

THE MANSFIELD SANCTUARY

Outside the sanctuary, Jackson quickly gets out of the car. Running towards the entrance, he opens the doors for Charlie and John to bring Carolina's limp body inside. He yells out to anybody who might help, "Please, somebody, get a doctor. My son has been shot in the head. Get somebody to help my boy." Two white male orderlies soon arrive and place Carolina on a gurney to rush him into an emergency room. Jackson, Charlie and John follow closely behind.

Jackson enters the room with Carolina. Charlie and John stay just outside the emergency room door. Shortly after, a white doctor and nurse enter the room, and their facial expressions change to disapproval when they see that Carolina is a black man. Jackson could see the bigotry on their faces as they hesitate to approach Carolina. Jackson angrily lashes out, "What is it? You've never seen a black man before? Don't just stand there. Can't you see that my son has a bullet in his head? Do something." The doctor quickly and nervously moves to examine the gunshot wound. He curtly speaks to the nurse, "Come and clean the wound. I need to be able to see the damage!" He looks at Jackson and rudely says, "You'll have to leave." Jackson angrily stares at him and responds, "Sir, I'm not being disrespectful, but I can't do that. For the sake of my son, I think I better stay with him." The doctor can tell by the look on Jackson's face that he better not insist any further. Then the doctor, putting on a pair of magnifying glasses, examines the wound. Looking at Jackson with a puzzled look, he says, "I don't understand why there is no bleeding! Normally, there is a lot of bleeding from a bullet wound. It appears that the bullet has gone too far inside to be removed. Your son will die if we perform surgery. There's nothing we can do for him, and he may never come out of the coma." Jackson's look of anger has turned into grief as he replies, "I see. Since you can't or won't help my son, I'll take him home. I believe the power of God will bring him back."

Jackson leaves Carolina's room and goes to give his sons the news. He is surprised to see that everyone, including Harriett and his daughters, are waiting. He expected for the women to be at home. With sorrow in his voice, he says, "Carolina is alive. He's still unconscious and the bleeding has stopped. The doctor can't or won't help him. He said the bullet can't be removed because it's too far inside his head. I'm going take him home."

Harriett rushes into Jackson's arms and demands, "I want to see my boy!" With his arms around Harriett, he looks at his children reassuringly and says, "Carolina is going to be fine; although, he has a long recovery ahead of him." Jackson holding Harriett at arm length looks seriously at her saying, "What I need for you to do is go back home and get a down stairs room ready for Carolina. It will be best to wait until then to see him. The nurse is cleaning him up right now. Speaking of nurse, prepare a room for Nurse Matilda next to Carolina's room. Baby, can you do that for me? Girls, go back home and help your ma. Clifton, I need you and Ernest to take them home. Prepare the wagon with lots of quilts and a couple of pillows so we can lay him down. Dudley, find Nurse Matilda. Tell her to be at the house by the time we get Carolina home. Also, tell her that I'll pay whatever it will cost for her to stay around the clock to help get him well."

Primus, looking very upset, insists, "My Pappy, the rest of us will wait here with you." Jackson looks at him and gently says, "Primus, if I leave Carolina here, they'll let him die. I believe God wants me to take him home. I believe that he will be with us for a while longer. God isn't ready for him. Son, believe what I'm saying. All of you must be strong and believe that he's going to come out of this. Now, I've got to go be with Carolina. I don't trust leaving him alone. Come and get me when Clifton and Ernest get back with the wagon." Clifton and Ernest are ready to take their ma and sisters home. Ernest insists, "Y'all, let's go and get things ready for Carolina."

Jackson's son, Carolina Fuller
(My grandfather)

1852 - 1919

CHAPTER 15

RECOVERY OF THE SHOOTING VICTIMS

THREE MONTHS LATER

It is early morning at Roscoe's parent's house, a small shack sitting on three feet blocks near the swamps. Inside Roscoe's small bedroom, his ma and pa are standing beside his bed watching him hallucinate. He's yelling, "Get off of me. Get him off of me. Stop. Stop. Don't hit me no more." His ma is putting a wet towel on his head trying to break his fever, "I don't know if Roscoe is going to have good sense with a bullet in his head and being kicked in the head the way that Fuller boy kicked him. It's been months and he still believes that he's being beaten."

His pa is standing there looking at him, "Roscoe has been looking for trouble for a long time. I'm surprise that he's still alive after bothering so many folks. If Bishop Fuller's son dies, we may as well dig Roscoe's grave. Nobody is talking. The police don't know who shot Carolina and don't seem to care. The Fullers' won't say a word about the shooting. Do you think they're going to kill Roscoe, and this is why they are not talking?" Roscoe's ma is now washing his body and changing his clothes, "I don't know. I just know I don't want my boy killed. When or if he gets better, we've got to send him away up north to live with your brother. You know, those Fuller boys will probably put an end to him."

Over at Jackson's house, the daughters, Alice, Dilsie, Gracie and Mimie are washing and hanging sheets on the clothes line. John has just driven up in the front yard. He gets out of his car and follows the sound of his sisters laughing and talking in the back yard. Unnoticed, he sneaks up behind the hanging sheets, removes a white one from the clothes line and covers himself. Making a growling sound, he leaps towards them. The sisters scream and Mimie reaches for a rake lying nearby to hit whoever is underneath the sheet. Dilsie quickly grabs the rake from Mimie. She recognizes the voice behind the growling, "John! I know it's you. I'll give you one minute to remove the sheet, or I'm going to put you in a coma." John stops acting crazy and removes the sheet while laughing. He responds, "Dilsie! I didn't know you had it in you to put somebody in a coma?" Alice and Gracie were not afraid. They knew it was John.

John hangs the sheet back on the clothes line, "I didn't expect to see y'all up and working hard so early in the morning. Have y'all had breakfast? If not, I would like take all of you to Ruby's café. It's been hard on you girls since Carolina has been sick. Y'all need to get away for a minute." Alice responds, "It's a nice gesture, John, but we can't leave ma. She's not quite herself since Carolina got shot. With My Pappy being so busy taking care of his business affairs, we need to stay close to the house. He left early this morning to go look at some more land that he's interested in purchasing."

Dilsie is happy to see John, "Did you know Gracie is leaving next week to go to college to become a teacher? She's going to Houston, Texas. Mimie stops working, "John, I want to be a teacher, and I think I'll be a good one. My Pappy said so." Gracie looks at Mimie, "He's right. You like to study, and you'll be great at teaching."

Nurse Matilda walks out of the house and is standing on the back porch. She sees John and discreetly unbuttons a few of the top buttons on her nurse's dress. She has always had a crush on John since they were kids, "Good Morning John! It's a lovely day isn't it? Carolina is getting better. He's trying to come back to us. He spoke a few words to me this morning, and he knew who I was." John's gets excited when he sees Nurse Matilda. He's looking at her with a big grin across his face, "Good morning Nurse Matilda. I know that you're taking good care of Carolina. There is no nurse better than you. I believe you're as smart as old Doc. I'm glad to hear Carolina is beginning to come around. Why don't you go inside with me to check on him?"

John goes into the house, and Nurse Matilda follows him. He opens the door to Carolina's room, and she rushes around him and goes over to Carolina's bed to adjust his pillows. Carolina opens his eyes a little and looks at John and smiles. John is happy that Carolina recognizes him, "Man, you've decided to come back from the dead. I've been praying real hard for God to wake you up. It's been three months. Every night My Pappy sits by your bed for hours anointing you with blessed oil and thanking the good Lord for bringing you back. Carolina, you'll be yourself in no time." Carolina is still very weak and cannot say much. He's reaches for Nurse Matilda's hand, "Nurse has been real good." He's holding her hand tightly, "Thank you." He smiles again and goes back to sleep. John looks at Nurse Matilda, "You're doing a great job taking care of Carolina and he's aware of it." John goes around the bed and hugs Nurse Matilda. She giggles and pats him on the back.

TWO YEARS LATER

It's mid-afternoon at Carolina's house. Carolina and Jackson are sitting in the living room talking. Jackson is sitting opposite Carolina in a big wide wing comfortable chair, "Son, I've been thinking. God has been good to you. He brought you back from a critical place near death. You are blessed to be alive. There's no more time for fighting and shooting. It's time for you to settle down and start a family. I've been told that Annie Farris has been spending some quality time with you since you've been home. You know, Ms. Annie is a fine looking woman, but she looks white and that can be dangerous. She's a black woman but white men don't know that she's black. They'll surely kill you if you are seen anywhere with her. Son, if you're thinking about marrying Annie, you can't take her into town or be seen together on these isolated country roads." Carolina has a serious look on his face, "My Pappy, you're right. I do plan to marry Annie, and I've thought about all the things that you've just said. She's been real good to me while I've been recovering, and I believe she will make me a good wife. She comes over every day with food, and helps me in every way that Nurse Matilda does. You know, I believe Nurse Matilda is jealous of Annie helping out the way that she does. Those two have never gotten along even when we were kids. I think it is time to stop Nurse Matilda's services? My Pappy, I don't want to hurt her feelings by telling her that I don't need her anymore. I think you should tell her since you hired her." Before Jackson could answer, there's a knock at the door. Jackson gets up and opens the door, "Hello Annie! Come on in. We were just talking about you. Carolina was telling me how you're taking good care of him." Annie enters the house carrying food, "Good afternoon, Bishop. I brought dinner for Carolina, and I made his favorite dessert, a peach cobbler." She walks over to Carolina, kisses him on his cheek and goes to the kitchen.

Jackson remains standing while watching her go to the kitchen, "Well, it's time for me to leave. I believe you and Annie can appreciate some quiet time together. Son, think about what I said. Don't worry about Nurse Matilda. She's done a fine job in caring for you, and I can see you're in good hands with Ms. Annie. I'll talk to her and let her know that her job is done. Don't get up, I can see myself out." Carolina doesn't obey his pa. He gets up and walks Jackson out to the porch, "Thanks, My Pappy, for coming by. I appreciate everything that you said about me and Annie. We'll be asking you to marry us real soon."

Roscoe has recovered from the shooting incident. When he got well enough to travel, his parents disguised him as a woman to sneak him out of the area. He's living in the north where his uncle lives. The gunshot wound to his head left him partially paralyzed on the right side. He's married to a woman who looks almost identical to Annie Farris. Roscoe doesn't drink anymore and stays to himself. Rumor has it that he's a gentleman and has become a deacon in the church.

CHAPTER 16

WHITE MEN ASK JACKSON FOR PRAYER

Two white farmers are standing outside another farmer's front porch discussing the two year drought that is threatening their farms. The owner looks at the other two men and asks, "What can we do about getting water for our dying crops? We can't afford another year of this drought. We'll lose the farms." One of the other two men sits on the porch. He removes his hat, scratches his head and says, "I'll do anything to save my crops. But, what can we do without rain?" Then the third man joins the man on the porch, and sitting next to him, he lets out a sigh and says, "Well, you all might think this sounds crazy. But, one of my workers, Willie, told me about this nigger preacher called Bishop Jackson Fuller. Supposedly, when he prays, God answers him and also gives him true visions. I was told that his crops are flourishing during this drought. Rumor has it that a big rain cloud comes and drops rain on his crops and then it disappears. Maybe we should go ask him to pray for some rain clouds to come over our crops." The man sitting next to him responds in anger, "That's a bunch of hog wash. There isn't any nigger around these parts or anywhere else with power like that. If he has so much power, why doesn't he change his skin color from black to white? I don't believe that story." The third man responds, "Believe what you want. I believe what

Willie tells me about the Bishop. Willie may be a nigger, but he tells the truth. He even told me that the Bishop drives a fancy car, lives in a big white house like rich white folks, and has over 860 acres of land enriched with gas and oil." Finally, the irritated owner speaks after listening to the other two baffling on his porch about this black-magic Bishop, "Okay, I've heard enough. It all sounds farfetched. What do we have to lose? Should we go talk to him? Since, he's supposedly a man of God, maybe he'll have mercy on us even though we're white." They agree to go the next morning to Jackson's house.

The next morning at approximately 7:00 a.m., the three white farmers ride in a wagon headed up the tree-lined road towards Jackson's house. They get out of the wagon and go up onto the porch. One of the farmers knocks on the beautiful glass wood-framed door. Harriett is preparing breakfast when she hears the knock. As she walks to the door, she wonders who could be knocking so early in the morning. She looks through the sheer curtains hanging on the door and sees the three white men. She speaks through the door, "What business do you have here so early in the morning?" Nervously, the farmer who knocked answers, "Ah (pausing), yes ma'am we came to talk to the Bishop. Ah, we don't mean any harm. We heard that God answers his prayers, and we need him to pray for our crops." Harriett has a look of disbelief on her face as she answers, "Bishop is in bed. Why don't you men have a seat on the porch! I'll wake him." The farmer responds. "Yes Ma'am." He walks away from the door shaking his head in disbelief that he just called a black woman ma'am, and says, "She has a lovely voice. I wonder if she's pretty. Am I dreaming? Here we are sitting on a nigger's porch at 7:00 in the morning waiting for him to pray for us. I don't believe this." One of the other farmers can't believe what he just heard his friend say, and with a look of amazement says, "While we're here, I don't think you should talk like you're talking. What if she's listening?"

Thirty minutes later, Jackson opens the front door and steps out onto the porch. He's curious and somewhat irritated about being awaken so early. As he sternly looks at each one of the three farmers, he says, "I'm Bishop Jackson. Explain to me why you're at my home at this time of the morning and who sent you?" The farmer who knocked can clearly see that the Bishop isn't happy about being awaken, so he nervously says, "Ah, sir, we apologize for waking you. We have a critical problem because of the drought. Our crops are dying and we are about to lose our farms. Willie McCoy told us how you pray to God and he answers all of your prayers. We would like for you to pray for rain to save our crops." Jackson clears his throat. (He's trying to keep from laughing, because he can't believe there are three white men at his house asking him to pray for rain.) Realizing that it must be difficult for them, he graciously replies, "Well, I've been asked to pray for many things, but I've never been asked to pray for rain. Where did you men come from?" The other farmer who was so irritated just the other day, stands up and walks closer to Jackson, and says, "Sir, our farms are south of Mansfield. It took us a while to get here..." Jackson stops him from speaking any further. He says, "As a servant of God, I can't refuse to pray when I'm asked to do so. While I'm praying, it is important that all three of you believe that God is going to make it rain. Without faith, God will not answer. I want all three of you to stand before me with bowed heads and agree with me as I pray."

Jackson raises his arms towards heaven, closes his eyes and begins to pray,

"Father, we are standing here in agreement that whatever we ask you for, in the name of your son, Jesus, that you'll grant it. Lord these farmers' crops are dying from lack of rain. In Jesus name, I curse the drought. I ask Lord that you will send rain to save their crops and all the other farmers' crops. Bless each one of these men, father, with compassion toward their brothers regardless of the color of their skin. Teach them lord to speak kindly of their brothers and not to regard one man higher or lower than another. Show them lord that you created all of mankind equal and that you are no respecter of persons. Bless them Lord. Thank you for what you are going to do. Amen".

1852 - 1919

The farmer, who knocked on Jackson's door is no longer nervous in Jackson's presence, and wants to hug him but feels that it's inappropriate; so, he offers his hand and says, "Bishop Jackson, I've never heard anyone pray like you. I felt something go all through my body. Thank you for that powerful prayer." Jackson shakes his hand, and replies, "You're welcome. And may the good Lord bless your crops." The other two farmers are also touched by Jackson's prayer, and they also shake his hand and thank him. Finally, one of them speaks, "That prayer was powerful Bishop. I believe rain is on the way. I'm honored to have met you."

Three days later, a rain storm came and saved all of the farmers' crops throughout DeSoto Parish.

CHAPTER 17

KKK'S 1ST ATTEMPT TO KILL JACKSON

Jackson is expensively dressed in a wide brown hat, grey shirt and pants with a fancy brown belt and matching boots. It is early afternoon, and he's riding his favorite Clydesdale horse down an isolated rode on his way to visit Joshua. Riding very slowly, he thinks about how God has blessed his life. He stops suddenly as he sees several Klansmen coming towards him blocking the narrow road up ahead. Then, Jackson hears God clearly speak to him, **"Stand still. Remember my word. When the enemy comes at you from one direction, I will make them flee in seven ways."** (Deuteronomy 7:28)

The Klansmen have reached Jackson, and the first to speak is chewing tobacco and staring at him. He spits some tobacco out of his mouth and says, "Nigger! Where are you headed? That's a mighty fine horse you're riding. Why don' you get off of it and walk to where you're going. I can use an expensive horse like that for myself. When you get down, take off that fancy hat, belt and those fine boots. I believe I might be able to wear them."

Jackson doesn't show any fear; instead, he tilts his hat back and stares at them, then says, "I don't want any trouble from you boys. I'm minding my own business, and I strongly suggest you boys go and do the same. The horse, hat, belt and boots are mine. Now, you tell me why I should give them to you?" The Klansmen find his words amusing. They start laughing and are eager to put their hands on him. A second Klansman defiantly says, "Well now, it looks like we have a smart mouth nigger here. What should we do with him?" They all dismount from their horses, and the third Klansman speaks angrily, "Let's rope this nigger up to one of those trees over yonder, and then let's see how smart he talks. A nigger like this one needs to be taught a lesson." Jackson sees a car speedily approaching from behind the three men and emphatically says, "I think it would be best if you boys get back on your horses and go about your business. I'm not getting off of my horse. You'll have to kill me right here. Don't you boys know that God protects his own? I belong to him!" Jackson now has a smile on his face, and the Klansmen are very angry and puzzled by Jackson's confident behavior.

As the Klansmen get down from their horses and walk toward Jackson to take him off of his horse, the approaching car stops so fast that the tires skid and make a loud noise. Jesse, Rochelle and Clifton quickly get out of the car. Jesse has a rifle in his hands that's aimed directly at the Klansmen. He calls out, "My Pappy! Looks like you can use some help. We'll take it from here. Are you red necks about to do something? You want to tell me what that something is? This is our pa, and if you want to hurt him that means you want to hurt us." Rochelle, has a pistol in each hand, and is aiming them at the Klansmen. He angrily asks, "Jesse? Should I shoot these bastards right now? My Pappy, why don't you leave? You don't need to see what we are about to do." Jackson finds it difficult to keep from laughing as his sons stand there ready to kill for him. He knows God sent them and insists, "Sons, I don't think y'all need to kill these evil men. One day their own evil will destroy them. Don't do any harm to them. Let them go." The three Klansmen tremble with fear near Jackson's horse, and one of them pissed in his pants.

Clifton walks up to one of the Klansmen and places the tip of his rifle on the side his head. Not looking at his pa, he says, "My Pappy, I'm going to blow this one's brains out right now. Second thought, I don't have to shoot him. I should beat him like he's never been beaten before. Then, they all will know not to mess with you or any other colored folks in these parts." Jackson looks seriously at him and warns, "Clifton, I taught you better. Let these devils go." He looks at the Klansmen and insists, "Get on your horses and get out of here before my boys stop listening to me." Rochelle with both of his pistols still aimed at them yells, "Go on and get your red-neck asses out of here before we kill all three of you and apologize to our pa later." The Klansmen rush to get on their horses and quickly ride away without looking back.

1852 - 1919

Clifton asks, "My Pappy? Where were you going? You shouldn't be going nowhere without one of us with you. You know the Klansmen will lynch any colored man they see alone on these roads." Jackson looks at his youngest son and replies, "I was on my way to visit Joshua. He's been under the weather." Jesse puts his rifle back into the car and adds, "We are on our way to Mansfield. My Pappy, we'll follow you back home. I'll come later and take you to see Joshua." Jackson turns his horse around to return home and agrees, "That's a good idea. Sons, I'm glad y'all came when you did. It had to be God who sent you."

Jackson's sons follow him home. When they all arrive there, Jesse and Rochelle talk in secret. They don't want Clifton or Jackson to hear them. Jackson and Clifton have gone into the house, and Clifton is in his room packing. He has to leave later in the day to go back to college in Houston, Texas where he's studying to become a teacher. Rochelle whispers to Jesse, "We need to do something about those red necks that wanted to hang My Pappy." Jesse agrees, "Yeah, we've got to do something. Let's go find those pecker woods and get rid of them. What's going to happen if they see one of us alone? We need to get rid of them before they get rid of us."

When Jesse and Rochelle get in the car to drive to Dudley's house, Jesse constantly looks through his rear mirror to make sure no KKK are following them, and says, "Rochelle, it would be easier if there were four of us. What about John? We can't involve Carolina. He can't afford to get hurt again." Rochelle is still angry about the Klansmen threatening to kill Jackson, and replies, "You better think again. John is too good to do the type of damage that we need to do." Again, Jesse agrees, "Yeah, you're right. Then, we'll ask Ernest." Rochelle looks at Jesse and adds, "Okay. After we leave Dudley's, let's go tell Ernest what happened and see if he wants to help us get rid of those bastards. Do you think you know where they live? You said you've seen them before?" Jesse answers, "Man, I believe they live near old man White. When I was delivering him corn last month, I saw those three Klansmen watching me like they wanted to do some harm."

Jesse drives up into Dudley's yard and repeatedly blows the horn for Dudley to come out of the house. Dudley soon comes out of the house yelling, "Stop blowing that horn. You're going to wake the baby. What's going on, Man? Y'all look and act like somebody is after you."

Rochelle, sitting on the passenger's side, looks through the window at Dudley, and replies, "Dudley, you won't believe what happened this morning. My Pappy was on his horse riding to Joshua's house and was stopped by three Klansmen. They were getting ready to take him off his horse and hang him. Jesse,

110

1852 - 1919

Clifton and I drove up just in time to stop them. We want to know if you will help us kill those bastards. If we don't handle this, they will kill one of us the next time they see one of us alone." Dudley is shocked to hear this news, and asks, "Is My Pappy alright?" Jesse answers, "He's fine. We saw him safely home." Then Dudley asks, "What do you have in mind? Surely you know that you're going to have to kill all of the Klansmen. Otherwise, there will be serious retaliation. Y'all best think hard about all of this. Also, keep in mind that My Pappy is close to God. Anybody who tries to do harm to him usually find themselves in pretty bad shape afterwards. God seems to fight for him in a vicious way. Y'all might not have to do anything. We should wait a little while, and see if anything strange happens to them." Rochelle nods his head in agreement, and responds, "You're right. Remember what happened to that white man who was shooting at My Pappy when he was driving his car to Shreveport? He had a heart attack and died right in front of pa's eyes." Jesse adds, "My Pappy did tell those red-necks that their own evil would one day destroy them. Maybe he said that because he was seeing a vision. So far, all of his visions have come true."

Harriett and Jackson relax in front of the fireplace after a day full of activity, and Clifton has since gone back to college in Houston. Enjoying their time alone, Harriett sits in a large chair admiring Jackson as he intently watches the fire. She asks him, "Why

111

are you so quiet? You must have serious thoughts going through your head." Jackson, gazing at Harriett and thinking she is beautiful with her hair hanging down, quietly replies, "I was thinking about the boys. This afternoon I was on my way to visit Joshua. Three Klansmen stopped me and threatened to take my horse and strip me naked. And, when they got off their horses to hang me, our boys drove up just in time to stop them." Jackson is troubled that his boys were carrying guns, but adds, "If the boys didn't have guns, the KKK would have tried to kill all of us. I know God watches all things and can stop anything from happening. But, you know, Harriett, far too many white folks hate us. They hate us because God made our skin black. What if God is Black? When white folks die, what are they going to do then? I'm beginning to think that living in a world where there is so much hatred toward us black folks; maybe it's a good idea to carry a weapon. Don't we carry guns for dangerous animals when we're in the woods? Well, most whites are more dangerous than those animals. For protection, maybe I should carry my pistol wherever I go. In the Bible, God's army carried swords, and even David used a sling shot!"

Harriett gets up and goes to sit on Jackson's lap. She looks at him seriously and says, "Baby, why are you just now telling me what happened this afternoon?" She kisses him on his forehead while he caresses her back and unbuttons her dress. Finally, he answers, "I

1852 - 1919

didn't want thoughts of what happened to worry you all day." She stops kissing him and scolds, "Please don't ever hesitate to tell me anything that happens like that. I'm not a child. I don't know what I would do if something terrible happened to you. I love you so much. If you ever feel the need to carry a gun, I believe that you should. So far God has been guiding and protecting your every step. Listen to your heart. You'll know the right thing to do. I'm so grateful that the boys came when they did." She then unbuttons his shirt while kissing him on this face, neck and chest. Jackson becoming more aroused, smiles and asks, "Honey, don't you think we should take this upstairs?" Harriett is too excited to stop and eagerly says, "Why not be a little adventurous? Our children are grown and gone." She continues to undress him, and Jackson surrenders to ecstasy.

1852 - 1919

ROCHELLE FULLER

JESSE FULLER   **CLIFTON FULLER**

CHAPTER 18

KKK'S 2nd ATTEMPT TO KILL JACKSON

ONE MONTH LATER

It's around 7:00 p.m., fourteen Klansmen, wearing white sheets and holding torches, wait for the Grand Wizard in a wooded area. They're telling nigger jokes when the Grand Wizard rides up on his horse. He gets off, goes and stands in front of them, and begins to speak, "I've called this meeting because we have a problem with some niggers who got out of place with my three boys last month. These are not ordinary niggers that I'm talking about. I'm sure y'all have heard about the Fuller niggers. The father is a Bishop. He has nine boys who don't know the meaning of fear. They have lots of money, live on a lot of land, and we need to destroy them and what they have. We've got to teach niggers around here that they can't disrespect a white man." The Grand Wizard pauses and looks at them as though he expects some type of rejoicing; but, they all stand speechless, so he continues speaking, "Come Saturday night, I want y'all to meet at my place at about 7:30 p.m., as soon as it gets dark. All of you are to bring your weapons and a can of gasoline. We're going to the Bishops big house to burn it to the ground. If any of them run out of the house, shoot to kill. There is only one safe way to do this. We will have to enter the woods behind the house, and we'll leave the same way. I'll carry the largest torch to guide us through the woods."

Next morning, the Grand Wizard's youngest son knocks on old man White's door. Mr. White opens the door and asks indignantly, "Boy, what you want this early?" The boy answers, "Howdy, Mr. White! I need a can that will hold some gasoline. There are lots of them in your back yard. I'll bring it back when I'm done." Mr. White is curious and asks, "Boy! What you need a can of gasoline for?" Rubbing his chin and wondering if he should tell the truth, the young boy answers, "I suppose I can tell you. But, you can't tell anybody. Pa will hurt me if he finds out that I told you." Mr. White becomes impatient and snaps, "Boy, if you want the can, you best tell me what you want it for or leave." The young boy is eager to get the can, so he confesses, "Okay, I'll tell you. Please don't say a word to no one. Come Saturday night, Pa and the other Klansmen are going to go to that Bishop nigger's house and burn it down. If anybody comes out of the house, they'll be killed. I can't wait. Pa is going to let me go with them." Old man White's face turns as white as the sheets that the Klansmen wear, and swears, "My God! I won't tell a soul. I know how evil your pa can become. Go on and get the can." With the look of a conspirator, old man White shuts the door. Once the boy leaves, he saddles up his horse and rides off to Jesse's house so fast that he can hardly stay in the saddle. When he gets to

116

Jesse's, he hears the chopping of wood coming from around back. He gets off his horse and rushes towards the back yard frantically yelling, "Jesse! Jesse!" Jesse stops chopping the wood when he hears Mr. White. He waits for the old man to come to the back yard. Immediately, Jesse asks, "Mr. White, what brings you here?" The old man was sweating so much that one would think the horse rode him. Out of breath, he finally answers, "Jesse, you and your family have been real good to me, and I want to return the favor. I got a visit this morning from the Grand Wizard's son. The Klansmen are planning on burning Bishop's house down come Saturday night. He said they're going to kill anybody who comes out of the house. You and your brothers have got to stop them."

The news shocks and angers Jesse; yet, he calmly responds, "Mr. White, thank you for coming here to warn us. It's best that you leave before they see you here. Don't worry, we'll handle the KKK. Again, thank you for coming."

Jesse is anxious to get the news to his brothers, so he decides to take a short cut through the woods to Carolina's house. He saddles up his horse and quickly leaves. Finding Carolina under a shade tree cleaning his rifle, Jesse says, "Carolina! How is it going man? I've come with some bad news. Old man White came by the house not long ago and said that the Wizard Master and his Klansmen are going

117

to burn down My Pappy's house and kill anybody who runs out of it. This is going to happen Saturday night. Today is Wednesday, so we don't have much time to come up with a plan to stop them."

Carolina doesn't look at Jesse right away; instead, he continues cleaning his rifle as if lost in thought. Finally he looks up and replies, "Well, Jesse, I guess I was cleaning my rifle for a reason. Man, that's serious. Okay, this is what must be done. We've got to get all the brothers and Uncle Stuarts two sons over here tonight around 7:00 to figure out a plan to stop those bastards. I'm going to go tell My Pappy what they plan to do. Clifton is away at school. So there are eight of us and two cousins – that's ten. It'll work. After I leave My Pappy's, I'll go and talk to Uncle Stuart's sons, Albert and Bob, to make sure they're here tonight. I'll let Charlie, Ernest, and Primus know. You go and tell Dudley, John, and Rochelle." Jesse gets back on his horse and confirms, "Okay. I'll see you tonight at 7:00."

Carolina drives up in front of his parent's big beautiful white house, and enters through the front door to find his ma and pa in the Kitchen. Harriett has just finished baking cookies, and Jackson sits at the table drinking coffee. Harriett is happy to see Carolina, and cheerfully says, "Son, it is so nice to see you this afternoon. You're looking real good. Annie must be feeding you well. Looks like you gained some weight." Carolina walks over and

1852 - 1919

kisses his ma on the cheek. Jackson, noticing the look of worry on his son's face, puts his coffee cup down and points for Carolina to sit at the table. As Carolina sits down, he replies, "Yeah, ma, I believe I've gained a little weight. I came by today to let you and My Pappy know that the Grand Wizard and his Klansmen are planning on burning down this house Saturday night and will shoot to kill anybody running out of the house."

Jackson stands and walks away from the table to look out the kitchen window towards the woods located behind his house. He's silent for several moments, then turns to look at Carolina and Harriett, and says, "This is serious." Carolina goes over to the window and looks out to see what his pa was looking at. Seeing nothing but the woods, he looks at Jackson and adds, "Yes, it's very serious. I want you and ma to stay at my house Saturday night. Both of you need to come over before it gets dark. All of us boys and two of Uncle Stuart's sons are meeting tonight to come up with a plan to stop the Klansmen. My Pappy, I want you to do what you do best and that is, pray for our protection." Jackson immediately protests, "Son, I appreciate what you just said. But, don't you think that I should meet with you boys tonight? I may be a man of God, and as a man of God, I have the right to protect my family." Carolina puts his hand on his pa's shoulder, and looking him straight in the eye, he insists, "My Pappy, you have eight grown sons who will fight this battle for you and ma. We don't want you to be involved with the KKK. I need you to stay with ma, Annie and the kids. Protect them while we take care of the Klansmen. Please let your sons handle this fight? Let us fight for you and ma!" Staring at Carolina, a smile crosses Jackson's face, and he proudly says, "Carolina! You've always been a fighter like your great grandpa Christopher Columbus. You're right. I'll stay and take care of the women and children. Harriet and I will come to your house Saturday afternoon; and, while I'm there, I'll be having a talk with God to guide and protect all of you in this battle with the enemy." Carolina adds, "Ma! My Pappy! You must know that your sons will never let any harm come to either one of you. I've got to go and tell the others what time we're going to meet tonight." Carolina kisses his ma goodbye and rushes out the front door.

It's 7:00 p.m. and the Fuller brothers with their two cousins are at Carolina's house gathered in his living room. Some sit and some stand as Carolina clears his throat to catch everyone's attention. He begins by saying, "Okay, we all are here, so let's put our heads together and figure out how we are going to stop those Klansmen. I've been thinking. Usually, the KKK come during the night when you least expect them. The best way for them to attack My Pappy's house is to enter the property through the woods behind the house. Otherwise, they'll be seen. I figure, we can set up a trap in the woods for them, and they won't know what hit them." Everybody in the room is in agreement with Carolina and voices their approval.

John has a confused look on his face, and asks, "What type of trap do you have in mind?" Carolina becomes more excited as he continues on about his plan, "Well, we are going to need a lot of rope, your guns with plenty of bullets, and a whole lot of "skunk oil." Also, we'll need plenty of buckets to fill with the oil." Charlie quickly responds, "There is plenty of rope in My Pappy's barn. I'll get it and bring it here tomorrow morning." Primus has a frown on his face and confesses, "You've lost me. Why on earth do we need "skunk oil? Does that mean we're going to have to go hunting for the skunks to make the stuff?" Dudley grins and responds, "Grandpa Carolina showed us how to make that nasty stuff. What are we going to do with it?" Smiling, Carolina explains, "Man, I've given a lot of thought to this plan. We are going to use the "skunk oil" to drop it from the trees on the Klansmen and their horses once they trip over the ropes. When they enter the woods, we will have ropes tied low to the ground around the trees. The horses will trip and fall causing the Klansmen to fall to the ground. This will trigger the other ropes that are attached to the buckets of oil, and the oil will spook the horses. That's when we'll attack them. Hell, those horses may do so much damage to the Klansmen that there might not be a need for us to do anything but watch. They won't be expecting us, and they won't know what hit them. What do y'all think about all that?" Laughing, Ernest shakes his head and exclaims, "Carolina! How in the hell did you come up with this plan? Man, it's brilliant. I believe that it will work." Primus laughs so hard that he starts gasping for air as he weakly says, "Well, I guess we better all get up early in the morning to go find us some skunks. Thank you Grandpa Carolina (looking up towards the ceiling) for teaching us about your "skunk Oil." More serious than the others, John adds, "Okay, the plan is great. Now, tomorrow is Thursday. Five of us should go hunting and make the oil. The rest of us need to start roping a wide-spread area of the woods where the Klansmen will most likely enter. Man, I believe this is going to work." Charlie gets up to leave and says, "It sounds like a plan. I'll be here early to help find those skunks." Almost out the door, Dudley calls over his shoulder, "Carolina! Shoo you're right. The plan is too good. We'll go get the skunks in the morning." Carolina is happy that everyone seems pleased with the plan and urges them on, saying, "Okay. So, let's all meet back here Friday evening at the same time to make sure everything is ready. I'll see you then." Walking towards the door, Ernest boasts, "All I've got to say is that, when somebody wants to hurt my ma and pa, there isn't anything I won't do to protect them. Let's get it on and kick those KKK asses." Jesse, heading towards the door, turns and goes and lays his hand on Carolina's shoulder. Playfully, he

1852 - 1919

says, "Carolina! Carolina! Ever since you got that bullet in your head, you're much smarter." He laughs as hard as he can and Carolina laughs with him.

Meantime, Jackson is at home in his office praying for his sons and nephews to have victory fighting the Klansmen. He's on his knees.

"Father, in Jesus name, I ask that you will guide my sons and nephews and protect them from the hands of the enemy. The Klansmen have plotted against me and my household. You've promised me in your word that you would make my enemies fall in any ditch that they dig for me. Let their evil desires be returned to them. I know that you will show my boys what to do and I thank you for protecting them. Amen."

He leaves his office, goes upstairs to his bedroom and finds Harriett almost asleep. He undresses and gets into bed beside her; and before closing his eyes, he quietly assures her, "Harriett! God told me that everything is going to be alright tomorrow night. He said that no harm will come to us or our sons and nephews." Harriett is so sleepy and tired that she can't speak. With closed eyes, she smiles and goes to sleep.

The next afternoon at Carolina's house, Harriet, Jackson, and Annie are standing on the porch watching Carolina and the others get their gear ready for the battle with the Klansmen. They all have their pistols, rifles and lanterns loaded up in a small wagon that one of the nephews will drive to the woods. Jackson wants to pray for them before they leave, and he calls out, "Sons! Nephews! Come closer so that I can bless y'all before leaving." They approach the porch for prayer, bow their heads, and Jackson begins praying.

"Father God, thank you for my sons and nephews that are standing before me. They're a gift from you to me. I have done my best for each and every one of them. Now, I thank you God for going with them to fight this battle with the most devilish men upon the earth today, the KU KLUX KLAN. Make these men standing before me more than conquerors. Give them the Victory by fighting the battle for them. Amen."

Jackson pauses for a while and looks as though he's listening to something. He laughs and speaks. "The Lord just spoke to me and said that he's with all of you, and that the battle is his and not yours. After y'all position yourselves in the wood, just wait and watch."

They get on their horses and ride away with Carolina in the lead, and the wagon following close behind. They all look back and yell. "Thanks My Pappy.

Thanks Uncle Jackson." Jesse yells. "We all are coming back with good news."

Jackson J. Fuller

"A PREACHER MAN WHO KNEW NO FEAR"
THE EYES OF DEFEAT FEARED HIM

CHAPTER 19

BATTLE IN THE WOODS

IT'S 8:00 P.M. SATURDAY NIGHT IN THE WOODED AREA BEHIND JACKSON'S HOUSE.

Jackson's sons and nephews are just about finished attaching all of the buckets of oil to the ropes in the trees. John gets on his horse and rides to the entrance of the woods to look out for the Klansmen. Around 30 minutes after waiting, he sees lit torches coming directly towards him. He gets on his horse and rushes back to the others to let them know, "They're coming, and they're headed directly where we thought they would." Carolina is excited and reminds the others, "When I make the sound of an owl, that's the signal to pull the ropes for the "skunk oil" to pour from the buckets. The moon is full and is providing enough light for us to put out the lanterns now."

Fifteen Klansmen enter the woods behind Jackson's house, and the Grand Wizard carries a large lit torch, proceeding as though being led by an invisible force into the trap. Jackson's sons and nephews can't believe what they're seeing. The intruders on horseback ride in a line of five men side by side, grouped in three rows. The first row consists of four Klansmen led by the Grand Wizard, and they're now within the roped area. Carolina gives the owl signal, and his brothers and cousins begin pulling the ropes for the "Skunk Oil" to pour down on the Klansmen. Their horses trip over the hidden ropes, and they crash to the ground. Some of the horses stampede, killing the fallen Klansmen while the others are burned by their own torches. The Grand Wizard is on the ground screaming because of the fire that is consuming him inside of his white sheet.

Jackson's sons and nephews hide and watch all of the Klansmen get destroyed without them having to do anything. One hour has gone by, and the Grand Wizard is dead along with seven other Klansmen. The seven surviving Klansmen are severely injured with burns and broken bones; they struggle to leave the woods on foot because their horses have either died or run away.

Carolina, remembering his pa's prayer and what he said about God fighting the battle, whispers to the others, "Let's not kill them. God has done what he wants done to them. It's time to head home."

Jackson, Harriett and Annie are sitting on the porch waiting for their return. It's around 11:00 p.m. when they hear the sound of horses and a wagon coming. Jackson stands up looking in the direction of the sounds, and he sees them riding fast towards the house. As usual, Carolina is leading the men as he yells out to his pa, "My Pappy! God fought the fight.

1852 - 1919

It's over. We didn't have to fire one shot. Those Klansmen rode their horses directly into our trap as though they were being led by an invisible force. Eight of them were killed by their horses or burned to death by their torches. The Wizard Master was burned to death by his torch when he fell to the ground. The horses that didn't die from the fall ran away after the Klansmen fell to the ground. The seven survivors are severely burned with broken arms and legs, and we decided not to kill them. They're wounded badly and will probably die before they can leave the woods. God fought the battle for us just like you asked him to do.

1852 - 1919

CHAPTER 20

HARRIETT'S DEATH

NINE YEARS LATER – 1915

Harriett is very ill suffering from cancer of the liver and heart failure. She's confined to the bed, and Nurse Matilda has been hired to take care of her.

Nurse Matilda is headed upstairs carrying a breakfast tray for Harriett. She is very worried and fears that Harriett is close to death. Entering her room, she puts on a cheerful face, and says, "Good morning, Mrs. Fuller. It's time for you to take your heart medicine and to eat breakfast. How do you feel this morning?" Coughing and looking very weak, Harriett answers, "I'm tired Nurse Matilda, and my heart seems to be getting weaker by the day. The medicine isn't working, and I don't have an appetite. Maybe I'll just have some juice." Nurse Matilda puts the tray on the small table next to the bed, and adjusts Harriett's pillows. Then she pulls Harriett up into a sitting position in the bed and says, "Mrs. Fuller, you need food to make you stronger. Try eating a little bit." Harriett weakly looks at her, and answers, "You've been taking care of me for months, and we've become good friends. I would like for you to call me Harriett." Nurse Matilda giggles and agrees, "I can do that, but only if you call me Matilda." Harriett heartily agrees, "Matilda it

130

is!" Attempting to make Harriett feel better, Nurse Matilda cheerfully suggests, "Girl friend, let's get you cleaned up and smelling pretty before Bishop comes home today. He's going be anxious to see you after being away at that church convention all week.

IT'S LATE AFTERNOON, AND JACKSON DRIVES UP TO HIS HOUSE.

Getting out of the car and entering the house, he calls out, "I'm home! Hello! I'm home!" Alice and Mimie are in the kitchen cooking. Hearing their pa's voice, they enter the living room where Jackson is looking at some mail on the lamp table. Alice rushes to him with her arms spread wide and hugs him, saying, "Welcome home, I was in the kitchen with Mimie cooking dinner. I've missed you My Pappy. I'm so glad you're back." Mimie joins in and puts her arms around Jackson and Alice. Jackson can see that Mimie is taking her ma's illness harder than the others, so he pulls her in closer and says, "It's good being home. I have been missing my family. Okay ladies, I want to know how Harriett has been doing while I was away. Alice, you go first." Alice reports on the day's events first, and says, "My Pappy, ma is becoming weaker. She is refusing to eat, and she's sleeping a lot. I think she's dying." Mimie looks at her pa with teary eyes and adds, "I agree with Alice, I believe she's going to leave us soon."

Hearing his daughters say that they believe their ma is dying almost makes Jackson cry; and fearing that they are right, he tries to comfort them, saying, "If the good Lord decides to take Harriett home, there's nothing we can do about that. But, one thing you must remember. Your ma will always be with us. She'll live on in our memories and in our hearts." Jackson climbs heavily up the stairs to Harriett's room, and finds Nurse Matilda sitting beside the bed and reading a book. When Jackson opens the door, he finds Harriett in bed with her eyes shut listening to Matilda. Seeing Jackson enter, Nurse Matilda rises and greets him, then walks out of the room. Jackson sits in the chair next to Harriett's bed, takes her hand and calls her name. When Harriett doesn't answer, he lays his head on her lap and quietly sobs. This awakens Harriett, and she rubs his hair and speaks, "Don't cry. Honey, don't cry. I'll be gone soon to be with the Lord. You must accept this and be strong for our children. I'll be out of this sick body. It's terrible to be trapped inside of a dying body." Then, she immediately drifts back to sleep.

HARRIETT DIES ON MARCH 25, 1915

HARRIETT'S BURIAL

After Harriett's funeral service, six of her sons carry her casket to the cemetery behind the church. Weak and crying, Jackson follows with his sons, Clifton and Ernest, supporting him. Nearby, all the Fuller children are followed by a huge crowd of people.

ALICE FULLER

1 YEAR LATER

Mimie hasn't worked as a teacher since Harriett died. She felt the need to stay close to home so she could look after her pa. Jackson sits at the table eating, while Mimie washes dishes. She glances over at him, and says, "My Pappy, you're not eating enough! Is something bothering you?" Jackson looks over at Mimie standing in front of the sink, and replies, "No, I'm okay. I just don't have much of an appetite. Maybe, it's time for me to get back into the swing of things and start doing some work. I've been slothful with my business affairs. Ever since Harriett left, nothing has been the same." Mimie stops washing the dishes and joins her pa at the table. Sitting opposite him, she observes, "I can tell you've been having a lot on your mind. Can we talk about it?" Jackson takes her hand reassuringly, and says, "Mimie, you're a beautiful young lady. It's time for you to go on and live your life, and stop hovering over me. I'll be just fine. You're a very smart teacher, and you need to start educating the youngsters. Your ma wants you to teach, and so do I. I've been thinking a lot about this house. It's too big for me. Children need to be living here. So, I'm going to ask Clifton if he would like to have it. He has a large family and the kids love it here. As for you, I would like to build you a house of your liking on the land that your ma and I gave you; and I'll build me a smaller house. What do you think?" Placing her hand on top of his and smiling, she

1852 - 1919

replies, "My Pappy, I want you to be happy. Ma loved you so much, and I know that she's looking down from heaven and doesn't want you to be sad. I agree that it's time for a change. Let's do it. I'll start looking for a teaching job as soon as possible. I think Clifton's family will love living here." Jackson's face looks like a heavy burden has lifted from him, and he adds, "Looking for a job won't be necessary. There's an opening at the Bethlehem school. It's yours if you want it. Mimie, we'll stay here until our houses are built. You let me know when you want to go look at the land to decide where to build and we'll go together. There's one thing that's very important to me. I don't want you living in a house by yourself far away from everybody. So, when you make your decision, it would make me happy if you choose to build close to one of your brothers." Mimie answers, "I wouldn't have it any other way." She gets up from the table, kisses Jackson on top of his head and goes back to cleaning the dishes.

1852 - 1919

Jackson and Harriett

CHAPTER 21

THE FAMILY'S BBQ

It's early in the morning at Jackson's house, and while Jackson's grandchildren play in the front yard, all of his children are in the back yard preparing for a BBQ for family and friends.

Clifton and Carolina barbecue the meat on big tin fire-burning cans that are covered with iron racks. The cans are filled with hickory nuts and oak wood to add flavor to the BBQ. Ernest, Charlie, Dudley, Primus and Jesse remove redwood tables and benches from wagons. And, while Alice and Mimie are busy putting table cloths on the wooden tables, Gracie supervises everyone, rushing from one point to another getting on everybody's nerves.

Gracie yells across the yard, "Carolina! Clifton! Too much smoke is coming towards the house. Can you move those BBQ cans further away?" Carolina scratches his head looking at her, and then he complains to Clifton, "How does she think we can move these hot cans? Has she lost her mind?"

Gracie now focuses on Jesse, and she yells, "Jesse, you need to sit the benches at the tables as soon as you remove them from the wagon. Don't stack them in one area." Jesse ignores her and keeps stacking the benches. He feels someone else should be assigned to placing benches at the tables; he continues unloading the benches.

Gracie heads towards Rochelle and John who are pouring fermented wine into large wooden serving barrels. She gets a cup and tastes it. Quickly, she spits the wine out of her mouth and looks at both of them and repulsively speaks, "My God, what are you guys thinking? My Pappy will have a fit with this wine being so strong. Rochelle, you know better. John, get some water and dilute it." She walks away.

Rochelle feels like pouring the whole barrel of wine on Gracie. Instead, he looks to John, and playfully says, "I think Gracie needs to drink a lot of this strong wine to calm her nerves. Her presence is making everybody nervous."

John has to laugh to keep from cursing, and complains, "She acts like she's in her classroom disciplining her students. Hell! What she needs to do is go somewhere and sit down. She's probably right about My Pappy. The wine is pretty strong. I'm going to dilute it a little bit. We can't have people getting drunk and acting crazy."

1852 - 1919

**The "BBQ Disciplinarian"
Gracie Fuller
Jackson's daughter**

ALL EIGHT DAUGHTER-IN-LAWS ARE IN THE KITCHEN PREPARING FOOD FOR THE BBQ. Their names are: Mertha, Annie, Dilsie, Mary, Lubirda, Henry Lee, Mattie, Katie, and Mattie. (Annie and Henry Lee are sisters.)

They're preparing vegetables, sweet potatoes, cakes, peach and black berry cobblers, Sweet Lucy cool-aid, BBQ sauce, potato salad, corn on the cob, bread, and other delicious foods. They have only one thing in common - their husbands, and each one has something to say.

ANNIE, putting frosting on a cake, says without looking up, "Ladies, I have a problem with **Carolina**. He's been coming home late at night. I don't know what's going on. But, I will get to the bottom of it. I believe he might be cheating on me."

MERTHA, stops from her biscuit making and responds, "Annie, you shouldn't think that unless you have some proof. You know how men like to hang out together drinking. **Clifton's** at home every night and it better stay that way."

MARY, seasoning the meat for the BBQ, glances up every now and then says, "Mertha, Clifton is still at home every night because y'all haven't been married long enough. Just wait until he gets use to you. He'll start sneaking like the rest of those hound dogs. **Jesse** and I have been married longer. He's a good man, but at church, I catch his eyes roaming here and there at some of those whores. You know they all flirt and want to have a Fuller man."

LUBIRDA, making peach and black berry cobblers, without looking up or stopping agrees, "Mary, girl, shoo you're right! All those whores around the church are after the Fuller men. Every time I look up, I see one of them in my man's face. I told **Primus** that he better follow in the footsteps of his pa, Jackson. I won't have a whorish man sleeping in my bed."

DILSIE, putting potatoes in boiling water, says, "Lubirda, you know a man will be a man. What you've got to do is give him enough rope to hang himself. When he gets caught, then you have to teach him a lesson by pouring hot water on him when he comes home late and goes to sleep. Just make sure that the water isn't hot enough to do serious damage. I've already told **Rochelle** that if I ever find out he's cheating; he can expect some hot water. You've got to put the fear of God in a man."

HENRY LEE, (Annie's sister) is stacking the plates and collecting silverware to take outside. She stops and reaches for a black skillet. Holding it up in one hand, she speaks, "Dilsie pouring boiling water on your man is darn right evils. You shouldn't do that to a dog. Why would you do that to your man? Breaking a plate over his head or hitting him with a black skillet will do the job. **Dudley** has had a few

141

skillets upside his head, and I don't have any more problems at all."

MATTIE, cooking black-eye peas, is slicing pieces of ham into the pot for flavor. She warns, "Okay, Henry Lee, that's enough. Today is supposed to be a day of happiness. Let's talk about the good things. If y'all keep talking like this, you're not going to be able to enjoy the BBQ. **John** and I have our problems, but we work them out. There are no perfect marriages. My mama says, when you have a problem with your man, put it in God's hand, and he'll fix it. It is not necessary to get physical."

LINDA, putting butter on steaming hot cobs of corn agrees, "You're right, Mattie, I love **Ernest**. He's good to me and the kids. I know that he loves us, and I know that he'll never look at another woman. There is no need to get physical hurting your man."

The sister-in-laws laugh and disagree with Linda.

MATTIE, chopping onions, bell peppers, boiled eggs, and celery for the potato salad, stops laughing and wipes away tears from the onions. Shocked, she responds, "Linda, I can't believe you said that. As long as men have eyes, they are going to look at what looks good to them. There is nothing wrong with looking as long as he doesn't stare. Hell, I look. I tell **Charlie** that he can look, but better not stare or touch."

1852 - 1919

Annie looks towards the entrance to the living room, and hushes everybody, "Change the subject, I hear Bishop coming down the stairs."

Jackson feels good as he comes down the stairs wearing a wide cowboy hat, fancy cowboy shirt with fringes, pants and snake skin boots. He walks into the kitchen and is immediately hit by the delicious aroma of food. Speaking to all, "It sure smells good in here. We're going to have a boot-kicking good time today. I've asked some of the ladies from the church to bring food – so there will be plenty to eat. The musicians from the church are going to play some dance music so you ladies can dance with your husbands."

The daughter-in-laws thank Jackson as he walks out of the back door.

The musicians from the church and nearby communities are playing music as the guests begin to arrive. Ladies enter the yard carrying dishes of food, while the men make a b-line toward the barrels of wine. Jackson makes his rounds, greeting all the guests, and the children are having fun a short distance away swinging on the swings that Clifton hung up on the trees.

Nurse Matilda enters the back yard looking very sexy. She's almost unrecognizable, wearing a ruffled low off-the-shoulder blouse that shows her cleavage. She sees John and immediately rushes to him, excitedly saying, "Hello, John. How are you? It looks like we're going to have a great time today." John is surprised by how sexy Nurse Matilda looks, and he stammers, "Hey Matilda! I almost didn't recognize you out of your nurse's uniform. You're looking mighty fine. Glad you're here." John spots his wife, Mattie, coming towards them, and he quickly dismisses himself, "See you later, Matilda." He walks towards Mattie and takes her arm leading her in another direction. Mattie has missed none of it, and accusingly says, "I saw the way you were looking at Nurse Matilda. I'm telling you right now. Don't be caught in her face again. She has always wanted you, and I'll be damned if you are going flirt with her today."

It's early evening and Jackson sits and watches his guests have a great time eating and dancing. He taps his feet to the rhythm of the music as a beautiful guest named Elida walks towards him. His heart starts beating rapidly and he feels a little nervous. She's recently been visiting his church, and even though he invited her to the BBQ, he didn't expect for her to come. Elida, carrying a dish over to the Bishop, smiles and says, "Hello Bishop Fuller. (She elegantly extends her hand.) Thank you for inviting me to this lovely BBQ." Jackson stands and shakes her hand. "Ms. Elida, I'm so glad that you're here. I was hoping you would come." Strongly attracted to him, she boldly replies, "Nothing could have kept me away. I brought an apple pie that I baked myself.

144

Do you like apple pie?" Jackson, smiling broadly says, "I most certainly do, and I look forward to eating a piece." Jackson can't contain himself, and it's obvious to anyone who's watching that he admires what he sees. It's certainly no secret to Elida, who politely dismisses herself, "Ah, I better go put the pie on the table and join the others. Again, thank you for inviting me." Jackson calms himself, and responds respectfully, "I'm glad that you're here. Enjoy yourself." He watches Elida walk away, and breaks out with a joyous smile again. Carolina walks up to Jackson laughing at him, and says, "My Pappy, if you don't stop staring at that pretty lady, people are going to wonder if you're alright. Who is she? Where did you meet her?" Being a little embarrassed, he answers, "Her name is Elida. She visited the church last Sunday, and I believe she lives in Mansfield. I didn't mean to watch her like I did, but there is something about her that I can't quite put my finger on. She's different. No disrespect to your ma. You know I loved Harriett, but she's gone. Son, I've been praying for God to send me a wife. It's not good for a man to be alone. When I saw Ms. Elida walk into the church, I felt God sent her there for a reason. I'm not saying that she's going to be my wife, but it is a possibility. God would have to show me clearly before I come to that conclusion."

Carolina's changes to a serious tone and assures his pa, "My Pappy, we all think that you need to find someone special. Ma has been gone a little over a year now. She would want you to be happy and not lonely. If you think you're interested in Ms. Elida, then you should get to know her and see if you want her to be your wife. She's a fine looking woman."

Not far from Jackson and Carolina, Nurse Matilda dances her way towards them, and it's clear that she's had too much wine. Jackson begins to laugh at her as she stumbles the last few feet. Out of breath, Matilda has difficulty saying, "Bishop the music is sounding real good. Would you like to dance?" Jackson laughs even more, and playfully says, "Nurse Matilda, I don't know how to dance. I'll leave the dancing for the dancers. Looks like you've had too much wine. I better keep my eyes on you. Promise me, that you won't drink anymore this evening. You're my favorite nurse, and I don't want you getting sick." She dances around Jackson, then around Carolina, and suddenly stops when she exclaims, "Bishop, you're my favorite preacher! Whatever you say – I will obey! Come on Carolina, let's dance!" Carolina knows better than to dance with Nurse Matilda because Annie is the jealous type. So he declines, "Nurse Matilda, you know if Annie sees us dancing, you'll have a fight on your hands. She's as jealous now as she was when we were kids." Nurse Matilda doesn't like his answer, and protests, "There's nothing wrong with dancing. I believe Annie is one of those people who like to fight. I'm a lover not a fighter – so, fine. I'll pass on dancing with you." She walks away and says almost too loudly to herself, "Annie, who does she think she is? That white looking bitch is always ready to beat up on folks."

All of the daughter-in-laws sit at the same table watching everybody have a good time. They're worn out from cooking, and their eyes follow their husband's every move. All that negative kitchen talk has them very suspicious.

The band is playing a slow song, so Carolina thinks he should ask Annie for a dance. He walks over to her table and reaching out says, "Annie, come on baby, let's dance." He pulls her up into his arms and starts dancing. Jesse, as always, follows Carolina and asks his wife Mary for a dance. "Mary, I've been waiting all night for this dance. Suga, let's show them how it's done." He swirls Mary around and pulls her close to him. Seeing Carolina and Jesse dance with their wives, the other brothers ask their wives to dance. They know that they will never hear the end of it if they didn't.

Jackson feels good and is glad to see that the BBQ is a big success. As he watches his sons dance with their wives, he looks at Elida sitting and chatting with some ladies. He is determined to get to know her. Nurse Matilda has found a dance partner. He's a deacon at Mt. Mariah. He's struggling to hold her up because she's drunk.

1852 - 1919

**Annie Farris Fuller
Carolina's Wife
(My Grandmother)**

CHAPTER 22

JACKSON GETS ENGAGED

It's mid-afternoon, and Elida has invited Jackson over for a visit. He's driving to Mansfield, and follows precise directions to her house. He gets out of the car with flowers, and before he can knock, Elida opens the door. She's wearing a beautiful dress and has a flower in her long pretty hair. Jackson notices that her perfume smells like roses, as she greets him, "Hello Bishop! Did you have any problems finding me?" Jackson replies, "As a matter of fact, you gave very good directions. I didn't have any difficulty." He hands her the flowers and says, "It's so good to see you." Elida graciously takes the flowers from Jackson, smells them and replies, "Thank you. These flowers are beautiful. Please, come in and have a seat. Would you like something to drink? I have tea and some coffee I just brewed." Jackson enters the living room and is admiring the décor, he replies, "Coffee sounds good. No cream. I like it black with a little sugar." Elida responds cheerfully, "Okay, make yourself comfortable while I put the flowers in a vase and get your coffee."

Jackson gets comfortable on the couch and patiently waits for Elida to return. As he's looking around, he can tell that she likes pretty dainty figurines. There are plenty of them on the fireplace mantle. She returns carrying a beautiful crystal tray with the coffee, and sitting down across from him, she shyly says, "Bishop! I'm so glad that you came. I've been thinking about you day after day. I hope you don't think I'm being bold by sharing this with you; but, for the past two months, I've been having many dreams about us as a couple. I've prayed and asked God to show me the meaning of them; but, I haven't received an answer yet."

Jackson is delighted to hear about her dreams. She has just made it easier for him to say what's in his heart, and he slowly begins, "Ms. Elida, thank you for sharing your dreams with me. Actually, I've been experiencing the same thing. I've been seeing us together as a couple in my dreams. I believe we were supposed to share our dreams today for confirmation that we are being brought together by God. I've been a widower for over a year; And, I'm lonely and have asked God to send me a wife. I think we need to find out if this is what God is showing us by dating for several months. Would you like that?" Elida expresses her pleasure, "Oh yes. I want to get to know everything about you. We can start by you not calling me Ms. Elida. Call me Elida." Jackson smiles, and with dreamy eyes, he accepts, "Okay, Elida it is, and I want you to call me Jackson. Elida is a lovely name for a lovely woman. Would you like to go for a drive? It's a beautiful day." They both start laughing and walk out of the house headed for the car.

CHAPTER 23

JACKSON FINDS AN OLD FRIEND

Shopping in a fancy ladies' boutique in Mansfield, Jackson looks for earrings, a necklace, and lace fabric for Elida's wedding dress. A sales woman stands behind the counter staring at him, because there has never been a black man in her boutique before. Jackson admires some lace, and noticing that she doesn't offer help, he calls out, "Ma'am! How much of this lace do I need to buy for a medium size lady's dress?" She stays behind the counter as she answers, "That lace is very expensive. It comes from France." Jackson is irritated by her attitude and insists, "Ma'am, I didn't ask you how much it cost. Can you tell me how much do I need to buy for a medium size lady's dress?" She is shocked and grudgingly responds, "Ah, I believe three yards will be enough; but, you'll need matching thread and buttons too." Jackson responds thoughtfully, "I hadn't thought about all of that. Those can be purchased later. I'll take the fabric and the beautiful pearl earrings and necklace that are on the counter." She looks skeptical, because she doesn't think he can afford what he wants; and, she walks proudly from behind the counter. She cautiously approaches Jackson to take the fabric for measurement, and returns to the counter to cut and fold it. She then removes the earrings and necklace from the display rack and places everything in a bag, saying challengingly, "Everything comes to $60.00." Jackson reaches inside his pocket and removes a hand full of coins. He gives her $60.00, and asks, "Will you please remove the items from the bag and wrap everything in some nice paper and then put it in the bag?" Shocked, the sales woman quickly replies, "Why of course. I have just the right wrapping for this purchase." She reaches underneath the counter and gets some pretty light blue wrapping paper. Business has been slow and she's happy to have made such a large sale. Attempting to make conversation, she starts, "She must be a special lady." Jackson doesn't respond and just looks at her.

Suddenly, the door opens and an elderly black woman rushes inside. She's wearing a beautiful bandana and a matching dress. She speaks to the sales woman with a beautiful accent, "Hello Ms. Judy, I'm sorry I'm late. I had difficulty getting here today. I'll get started right away unpacking the shipments." The woman goes to the counter and stands next to Jackson. She doesn't look at him as she talks to the sales woman. Her voice sounds very familiar. He tries to recall where he's heard it. Jackson looks at the woman and inquires, "Ma'am, what is your name? I believe I know you." She looks at him from his head to his feet and says, "Sir, you don't know me. My name is Sadie." Jackson quickly steps back a little ways from the counter and stares at her. "Sadie? Sadie from Dubois's Plantation? Sadie, it's me Jackson!" Before she can respond, he picks her up and swings her around. "Sadie, I never forgot you. I went back to the plantation looking for you, and no one knew where you had gone." He puts her down and she looks up at him. She can hardly talk, and breathlessly, she replies, "You're my boy, Jackson? My, my, what a fine looking man you've become. You look as though you're doing very well. I often wondered what became of you. You were such a smart boy. Jackson, my boy, I'm late for work. I wish I could continue to talk, but I need this job."

The sales woman is also the owner of the boutique. Standing behind the counter, she holds Jackson's bag with her mouth opened and eyes as large as silver dollars. Her day has been quite eventful. First, a black man comes in and purchases $60 worth of merchandise, and then she finds out that he's Sadie's son. Jackson quickly responds to Sadie, "You don't need this job anymore. I'll take care of you just like you took care of me. Sadie, I want you to come with me. Your working days are over." He looks directly at the sales woman and says emphatically, "Sadie won't be working here anymore." Then he turns to Sadie and offers, "Sadie, is there anything in this store that you would like to have before we leave? I'll buy you whatever you want." The sales woman has become emotional over the reunion, and tears begin running down her face. Sadie is also tearful and asks, "My boy Jackson, are you sure about what you're saying? You want to take care of me?"

Jackson takes her by the arm to leave and answers, "You were like a mother to me. Of course, I'm sure. Shall we go?" The sales woman quickly responds, "Sir, don't forget your purchase!" Sadie is so excited that it's difficult to understand her. As she puts her arm through Jackson's, she says on the way to the door, "Let's go, my boy, Jackson." She looks back at the speechless sales woman who is now crying and blowing her nose and says, "Goodbye Ms. Judy. My boy doesn't want me to work anymore."

Outside the boutique, Jackson leads Sadie to his beautiful car and opens the door for her. Having never been in a car before, Sadie feels very special. She nervously strokes the dashboard and the seats. Finally, she asks, "Jackson, are you a rich man? This is your car? Am I dreaming?" Jackson just laughs at Sadie and assures her, "No Sadie, you are not dreaming. Yes, this car is mine. God has been and is good to me. He is going to bless you with whatever it is you need or want through me. I'm so glad that I found you."

It's after church on Sunday afternoon, and Jackson asks all of his children to meet him at home. When they arrive, they all sit in the living room wondering why they're there. Detecting this, Jackson explains, "Looking at your faces, I can tell that y'all are curious why you're here. As you know, I've had another home built for me and one built for Mimie. Harriett and I always said that Clifton is to have this house to raise his children when we're gone. Mimie and I are going to move into our new houses within the next couple of weeks. I've asked Clifton if he and his family would like to live here, and he has accepted the offer. Do any of you have a problem with this decision?" Jackson looks at each one, and they each agree that Clifton and his family should have the house. Jackson smiles and says, "This makes me happy. It's a done deal. Now, understand that I'm only giving Clifton the house. All of the crops, cattle, and everything else on the property that generates income for the family is to stay the same. Sons, you've done wonders with the family business. Our income has gone far beyond my expectations. Keep up the good work." He then looks at each daughter, and adds, "Daughters, I'm proud of the excellent accounting you're doing for the family's business. God has blessed us with abundance not only for ourselves but to help others."

Putting his hands together and shifting from one foot to the other, he says to all, "Now, it is time for my happy news. I want you all to know that I've asked Elida to become my wife, and she accepted. We won't be having a wedding. There will be a simple ceremony at Rev. Brady's home. Nothing would make me happier than for all of my children to be present." John is the first to speak. "My Pappy, do you want me to be your best man?" Jackson agrees, "Of course, I want you to be my best man; and, I want the rest of my boys there to be the best man.

We're not going to do things the traditional way. I want to have nine best men." Then to his daughters he adds, "Daughters! Do either one of you have any objections to me marrying Elida?" Alice speaks first, "I believe I can speak for all of us. We have discussed Elida, and we feel that she is good for you. We know that you love her, and she seems to feel the same about you. We're happy for you." Jackson is pleased that his children approve and says, "That settles it. I'm getting married with all of your blessings." Quickly heading towards the stairs, Jackson says to his children, "I have a surprise. Give me a minute. I'll be right back." More curious than before, they ask each other what's going on. They don't have to wait long, as they hear their pa coming down the stairs with someone with him. All at once, they stop talking.

Jackson walks into the living room with an attractive elderly woman who is wearing a beautiful silk bandana and matching dress. She smiles at them as Jackson introduces her, "Sadie, these are all fourteen of my children." Sadie approaches each one and shakes their hand saying, "Pleased to meet you." They all are shocked to see this lady whom they've all heard so much about over the years.

Suddenly, they all speak at the same time. "My Pappy how did you find Sadie?...Welcome Sadie...We all are so glad that you're here Sadie!" Jackson laughs at them, and tries to return order.

1852 - 1919

"Okay! Okay! Stop talking at the same time! Don't scare Sadie away! Let me answer some of your questions. I found Sadie last week while I was shopping. I've asked her to come and live with me. I'm going to build some additional rooms onto my new house for her. She'll be living with me and Elida."

Mimie hugs Sadie and says, "Ms. Sadie, My Pappy often speaks good things about you. I'm glad he found you, and welcome home." Clifton takes hold of Sadie's hand, and adds, "Ms. Sadie, since there are so many of us here, I believe that I'll speak for all of us. My Pappy has told us how you both were brought together at a slave auction, and how you took care of him. I want you to know that we are glad that you're here. Welcome to our family."

Sadie happily responds to everyone, "My boy, Jackson, has told me about all of you. I look forward to getting to know each of you and all of your children. Thank you so much for welcoming me. I feel like I'm home. You're the only family that I have."

CHAPTER 24

JACKSON MARRIES ELIDA

It's early in the morning, and Jackson, Charlie, John and Primus ride their horses across the ranch checking their crops. They have good workers who come from throughout the parish. They stop riding when Jackson begins to speak, "I believe we're going to have excellent profits this year." Primus quickly responds, "My Pappy, every year the harvest gets better. We have good workers." Then Charlie adds, "Speaking of profits, My Pappy, we need to leave and go meet with those men in Shreveport about our profits from the gas. They want to add another pump on Jesse's land, and three more on Primus's land." John adds, "Oh! That reminds me, a man came by the house the other day to talk about drilling for gas on my land. He said he will be getting in contact with me soon. My Pappy, while you're there, you might want to ask someone about that." Jackson turns his horse to head home and finishes by saying, "Okay, I better go back to the house, so I won't be late for the meeting. John, I'll ask about the drilling on your land. Carolina and Jessie are going with us to Shreveport. Have a good day, and I'll see y'all tomorrow."

1852 - 1919

THREE WEEKS LATER

Jackson and his family are at Rev. Brady's house waiting for Elida to arrive for the wedding. Jackson is very nervous and his sons are probably just as nervous; their pa is getting married. As Jackson thinks about Harriett, he can't imagine how it will be living with another woman after living with Harriett for 45 years. He loves Elida, but it isn't the same kind of love that he had for Harriett. Alice interrupts his thoughts by rushing into the room announcing Elida's arrival.

Jackson and his sons take their position in the Reverend's large living room. Then the pianist begins playing the song for Elida to enter the room as Clifton checks his pockets for the large diamond ring his pa purchased for Elida. The wedding soon begins when Elida enters the room with her father. Wearing a beautiful lace dress made from the fabric Jackson purchased, she looks like an angel as Jackson watches her walk towards him. Elida smiles at Jackson as she walks up and reaches for his hand.

After taking their vows, the newlyweds jump the broom and rush out of the house as everybody throw rice at them. They get into a car that has "Just Married" painted on the back window, and tin cans tied to the back bumper, and drive away. Carolina and Jesse follow them until they get out of the rural area and onto a main road.

1852 - 1919

THREE YEARS LATER

Elida and Jackson have two small children one year apart in age. Their son's name is Roy, and the daughter's name is Ola V.

1852 - 1919

CHAPTER 25

JACKSON HAS A HEART ATTACK

Carolina drives up to Jackson's yard. Getting out of the car, he knocks on the front door and calls out to his pa, "My Pappy, it's me Carolina." Elida opens the door, and reaches for his arm, saying, "Hi, Carolina. Come on in. Your pa isn't feeling well today. He's taking a nap. Should I wake him?" Carolina is a little curious as to what's wrong, he answers, "No, Ms. Elida. It's not that important. What seems to be wrong with him?" She has a worried look on her face as she responds, "He's tired a lot and somewhat irritated. It's not like him to be that way. I've asked him to see a doctor but he refuses. Every time one of the children cries, he goes outside." Carolina looks towards his pa's room and asks, "Do you mind if I look in on him? I won't wake him up." Elida gestures with her hand for him to go and replies, "Of course not, go ahead."

Carolina quietly opens Jackson's bedroom door, and finds him sitting on the side of the bed staring out of the window. He quietly asks, "My Pappy, what are you doing? I thought you were asleep." Jackson turns to him and says, "Come on in, Son. I was asleep, and I heard a voice call my name. I was looking out the window to see if somebody was outside calling me. I heard the voice so clearly. I know I heard someone calling my name." Carolina,

161

still standing explains, "Ms. Elida said that you've been tired lately and a little irritated. Are you not feeling well? Do you want me to take you to see a doctor?" Jackson immediately answers, "No, I don't need a doctor. If God can't fix whatever seems to be wrong, then no one can. You know how I feel about the doctors around these parts. They'll let you die without blinking an eye. Shut the door. I want to tell you something that I don't want Elida to hear."

Jackson points to the chair for Carolina to sit down and begins, "Something strange is happening. For the past month, I've been seeing your ma, Harriett. Early this morning, I saw her standing over me smiling. She said she wanted me to go with her. I closed my eyes and opened them again, and she was still standing there. All of a sudden, she walked towards the door and disappeared. Carolina, as sure as you're standing there, your ma was standing over there on the other side of the bed. Son, I've heard people tell stories about their love ones coming for them. I'm beginning to think that my time is near and your ma is coming for me."

Carolina is really worried now and pleads, "Please don't say that My Pappy. Please don't ever say that again. God isn't ready for you yet. You're not an old man. What would we all do without you?" There is fear in Jackson's eyes as he looks at Carolina and he continues, "Don't say a word about this to your brothers or sisters. I don't want them to become worried. From the look on your face, I'm beginning to regret that I told you. I can't tell Elida about this. I had to tell somebody."

Carolina stands, and walks back and forth in the room; he stares at his pa and suggests, "My Pappy, why don't you get up and get dressed. Let's go for a ride. Maybe the fresh air will make you see things differently. Better yet, let's go get your favorite horse and ride through the woods. You always said that riding through the woods on a sunny day makes all of your troubles go away." Jackson stares out of the window again, and gratefully responds, "I know what you're trying to do, and I thank you. But, I cannot accept. I don't feel like leaving this room right now. I'll be alright. You go, and come back tomorrow. Maybe we can go for that ride then."

Carolina doesn't want to leave, but knows that his pa wants to be left alone. So, he reluctantly complies, "Okay, My Pappy, I'm going to go; tomorrow I'll be back. I have to admit that you've got me very worried talking about ma coming for you. I know that God isn't ready for you, and you've got to know that too."

Carolina leaves Jackson and drives to Alice's house. He needs to visit with her because she always makes him feel better. He only wishes that he could talk to her about their pa, but he promised not to tell anyone. Soon after, he arrives and sits in the car for a while. When he finally gets out of the car and knocks on the door, Alice opens it and says, "Carolina! I'm surprised to see you. Come in and have a seat. I just finished cooking. Do you want something to eat?" Carolina looks more worried than he intends, and he sits not saying a word. Alice notices that something is wrong and asks, "Why are you sitting there so quietly? Are you and Annie having problems?" Carolina answers without looking at her, "No, Annie and I are fine. I just left My Pappy and he told me some things that he asked me not to tell anyone. What he said has me feeling sad and I'm afraid."

Alice looks nearly as concerned as Carolina when she sits across from him and speaks, "Well, I think you better tell somebody before you lose your mind. What did he say? You know I won't tell." Carolina fearfully looks at Alice and suggests, "Maybe you should go visit him. He might tell you what he told me." The gravity of his words makes her teary eyed, and she insists that he tells her, "You best tell me. You know that I'm not a busy-body. I don't talk when I'm not supposed to. You can tell me anything and know that it's safe. You've got me worried. What's wrong with My Pappy?"

Carolina stands and starts walking back and forth like he did at his pa's. "Okay. I want you to go visit My Pappy." If he tells you, act like you've never heard it. He told me that he has been seeing ma, and that he believes she is coming for him. Ms. Elida said that he's been acting different. He's tired a lot and gets irritated easily."

Alice gets up from the chair and begins pacing back and forth. Finally, she says, "I don't like the sound of all of this. If anything happens to My Pappy, I don't know what I'll do. You think it would seem fishy to him if I go visit him today?" Looking at her, Carolina stops pacing and says, "No, don't go today. You know we have never been able to pull anything over on him. He'll know that I told you. Wait a couple of days. By then, he may be better. If not, then we all have something to be worried about."

Two days later, Alice and Mimie drive over to their pa's house. They sit in the living room talking to Elida when Alice asks, "Where is My Pappy?" Elida answers, "Your pa went to meet with someone at the church. He wouldn't say who he was meeting with or why." Alice looks concerned and asks, "Ms. Elida, how is My Pappy doing? I haven't seen him in a week. I've been so busy with school work. I have more students than I need." Elida sits and knits as she looks up at Alice, "Well, like I told Carolina, Jackson hasn't been himself lately. He doesn't have the energy that he normally has, and he easily becomes irritated. Lately, he acts as if he has a lot on his mind, and he won't tell me what is bothering him."

Mimie gets up from the couch and looks out of the window to see if she can see his car heading home. She wonders aloud, "Do you think we should wait for him? Maybe he'll tell one of us what's going on." Elida answers, "You're welcome to wait. However, he'll get upset if he knows that I've told you anything." Mimie assures Elida, "I promise you, we won't say a word. We'll act like we came by to pick up Sadie and didn't know that she had gone to Texas."

An hour has gone by before Jackson drives into the yard. Sitting quietly, they can hear him stepping up on the porch. He enters the house and says cheerfully, "Hello daughters! I saw Mimie's car and didn't expect to see you Alice. How are you girls doing?" Alice and Mimie answer at the same time, "Fine, My Pappy." Jackson looks at them with one raised eye brow. They know he's on to them, because he does this when he's suspicious. Finally, he says, "When you girls answer at the same time, you're up to something. Do you want to tell me what that something is?" With a fake laugh, Alice responds, "My Pappy sometimes you can be so suspicious. We didn't know that Sadie had gone to Texas. We came by to take her to spend several days or so with us. That's all." Jackson is more suspicious than before, so he challenges her, "That doesn't make any sense. I didn't ask you why you're here or anything about Sadie. I asked how you two are doing."

Changing the subject Elida asks, "Jackson, are you hungry? I fixed you a plate. It's in the oven." Jackson looks at Elida with a smile, and then he looks at his daughters again. Satisfied, he accepts, "I believe that I will have dinner. Will you ladies excuse me?" Again, Alice and Mimie answer at the same time, "That's fine, we're leaving My Pappy." Jackson now shakes his head, and repeats, "You girls are up to something. I don't know why you don't say what's on your minds." He laughs and goes into the kitchen.

TWO WEEKS LATER

Jackson and Primus are in Jackson's backyard gathering wood for the fire place. Jackson bends over with wood in one arm and suddenly falls to the ground. He clutches his chest in severe pain. Primus drops the wood in a heap, and rushes towards his pa who's lying on the ground in a fetus position and moaning. Primus tries to get Jackson up to carry him into the house; but, he needs help so he yells, "Elida! Elida! Come and help me. My Pappy is sick. Hurry up." The back door to the house flies open, and Elida runs out screaming, "Jackson! Jackson! What's wrong with him?" She helps Primus get him off the ground and into the house. Once in the bedroom, Primus quickly speaks to his pa, "My Pappy, you're going to be alright. I'm going to go tell Annie and Carolina to get over here and take care of you while I go get the doctor. I'll be back as soon as I can."

167

He runs out of the house and gets into his car. He drives to Carolina's house to send them to Jackson, and immediately leaves to go get the doctor. Carolina drives Annie to his pa's and quickly goes to tell the rest of the family what has happened.

THE NEXT DAY

Jackson has had a massive heart attack, and all of his children, grand children and daughter-in-laws are at his home. Elida sits at the kitchen table holding their baby boy, Roy, and says to Annie, "I'm really worried about Jackson. The doctor said it doesn't look good." Annie gets up and touches her shoulder saying, "Ms. Elida, all we can do is pray for Bishop. I made some herb tea. Hopefully, it will make him better." She walks out of the kitchen and heads back to Jackson's room. Carolina, coming out of his pa's room, meets Annie in the hall and suggests, "Annie, you must be tired. You were here all night, and this morning it took you hours to gather enough herbs to make tea for My Pappy. Baby, why don't' you go and get some rest. All of us are here, and we can manage without you for a while." Annie agrees, "You're right. I am tired. I'm going to go in the back and lay down. Come and get me if I'm needed."

Charlie and Ernest sit on the porch; Ernest looks as though he might cry says, "Charlie! Man I'm feeling real funny. I don't know if it's fear or what. I hope My Pappy is going to make it. He looks real weak to me." Charlie gets up to sit beside Ernest, and says, "All we can do is pray that God isn't ready for him yet. My Pappy has spent his whole life making life better for all of us and everybody else. He never took time for himself. I don't want to lose him. If only there was something we could do to make him better." Then, Ernest begins to cry; Charlie reaches over and hugs him.

1852 - 1919

Charlie Fuller

1852 - 1919

TWO DAYS LATER

Jackson's condition worsens. It's around 6:00 p.m. when he asks for Elida and all the children to come into the bedroom room. His heart is getting weaker by the moment, and he speaks very low, "I want each and every one of you to know that I love you. Elida, I've been seeing angels; and, I know one is coming for me at any time now. Take care of my babies, and I'm sorry that I have to leave you so soon. Boys, I could not have asked God for better sons. All of you have been a blessing to me; you made my heart glad. Be good and stay close to the Lord." Then, to the girls, he adds, "Daughters, my beautiful daughters, I love you all. Remember what I told you when your ma left. I'll live on in your memories and in your heart. I won't ever be too far away. Now, go and let me get some rest. Clifton, I want to talk to you alone." Everyone leaves the room except for Clifton.

Clifton sits next to his pa's bed and takes Jackson's hand. Jackson squeezes his hand, and looking at him with a distant look in his eyes, he begins, "Although, you're a man, Clifton, you're my baby boy. When you go home, go up to the attic. In the corner near the window, you'll see a barrel. In the bottom of it, there is some money. I put it there for your children's education." Jackson closes his eyes, and squeezes Clifton's hand tighter as he takes his last

171

breath. Clifton cries out as loudly as he can. "My Pappy! Don't leave me. Lord! Don't take him."

The other children are standing outside the bedroom door when Clifton cries out. They rush into their pa's room screaming and calling out for Jackson not to leave.

1852 - 1919

**CLIFTON FULLER
AND
HIS TWELVE CHILDREN**

CHAPTER 26

JACKSON'S DEATH

Jackson died March 7, 1919. He was 67 years old.

The news of Jackson's death spreads rapidly throughout DeSoto Parish, Louisiana, Houston and Dallas, Texas as well as other states in the south. On the day of Jackson's funeral, hundreds of people leave home early in order to be at Mt. Mariah Baptist Church for the service. Some people walk many miles, while others ride horses and horse drawn wagons filled with people. Whatever means of transportation available is used because very few blacks own cars in 1919.

The Ku Klux Klansmen feared Jackson after the incident on his land which killed the Wizard Master and others. Now, they rejoice at the news of his death. To them, Jackson was a man not to be reckoned with.

JACKSON'S FUNERAL

The funeral starts at 11:00 a.m. It is now 10:00 a.m.; Mt. Mariah's church bell is ringing as Ludd Flanigan slowly drives the black hearse, carrying Jackson's body, approaches the church yard. There is a large crowd of people in the church yard that can't enter

1852 - 1919

the church because it is already filled with people. The hearse makes its way towards the front door of the church through the crowd as they all move nervously out of its path.

Jackson's sons are waiting to remove their pa's body from the hearse. When the hearse finally stops near the church entrance, six of the sons remove their father's casket and slowly carry it inside the church. They place it on a narrow table in front of the pulpit where Jackson preached for 33 years. The sons take their standing positions: Carolina, Charlie and Dudley stand at the head of the casket, and Ernest, John and Primus stand at the foot of the casket. Clifton, Jesse and Rochelle sit in the front pew with Elida, Sadie, and their sisters. Wearing black suits with white collars, approximately fifty preachers from various cities and states sit in and around the pulpit.

Clifton cannot sit and watch as the mortician opens the casket revealing his pa's lifeless body inside. So, he quickly gets up from his seat and rushes out of the church followed by his wife. Jesse and Rochelle also get up, but to go stand with their brothers. Immediately, Sadie gets up and walks slowly to the casket to view Jackson's body. She rubs his hair and bends down to kiss his forehead. She doesn't cry; she goes and stands with his sons.

1852 - 1919

The musicians accompany the choir as they sing "Amazing Grace," and people throughout the sanctuary and the church yard are crying and screaming. Nurse Matilda is rushing around comforting those who have become hysterical. As she rushes by the open casket, she glances at Bishop Jackson and yells out, "Oh Sweet Jesus, Bishop is gone." Immediately, she faints and two men rush to carry her out of the church. A little later, Jesse returns to stand with his brothers and Sadie.

Due to the large crowd of people viewing Bishop Jackson's body, the service lasts about four hours. After the service, Jackson's sons carry his casket to the cemetery behind the church where his father, mother and wife, Harriett, are buried. A horn player leads the way playing "Swing Low Sweet Chariot."

Jackson was indeed an extraordinary man graced with courage, understanding, wisdom, and visions from God. He miraculously achieved unprecedented success because of his faith in God; he was respected by many people. Those who did not respect him feared him. Why? Because, they sensed God's presence or something powerful prevailed over his life.

1852 - 1919

BISHOP JACKSON FULLER'S GRAVE

CHAPTER 27

JESSE IS KILLED

The KKK returns to kill a Fuller eleven years after Jackson's death. They despise Jesse and target him because of his fancy suits, and the fact that he is always chauffeured around in a new 1930 Rolls Royce.

Jesse is seated in the back seat of his Rolls Royce on his way to Mansfield as the chauffeur, Joe, deliberately takes a wrong turn. He is taking Jesse to the Klansmen, because they have threatened to kill him if he doesn't. Suddenly suspicious, Jesse asks, "Joe, why are you taking Hwy 171? Man, I told you to take the back roads." Joe answers, "I'm sorry Mr. Fuller, I thought you said 171." Jesse notices Joe's nervous voice, and immediately knows something is wrong. He can feel it. He reaches in his boot and pulls out his pistol, and demands, "Man, I don't like going this way, and I know I never mentioned Hwy 171. Turn this goddamn car around and go the way that I told you to go." The chauffeur continues driving fast and weakly protests, "Sir, the road is too narrow to turn around. I'll have to go a little further up the road where it's wider. Jesse shifts in his seat nervously as the car stops, and the chauffeur shouts in mock surprise, "I'll be damned! Sir, there are Klansmen dressed in white sheets blocking the road up ahead. They're coming towards us." Jesse points

178

the gun at the chauffeur head, and orders, "You black ass bastard. You set me up. I should kill you now, but I don't want to waste a bullet on you. Put the car in reverse and get me the hell out of here." The chauffeur answers, "No Sir, I can't do that. They'll kill me."

There are approximately eight Klansmen dressed in white sheets. They're less than four feet from Jesse's car. Jesse begins shooting and kills three of them. One of the Klansmen shouts out at the chauffeur, "Driver, get your black ass out of that car, and get as far away as you can from here." The driver jumps out of the car and runs into the woods. A Klansman comes up from behind Jesse's car. He opens the door and pulls him out. They begin to beat him with iron bars and kick him in the head. Those who are not savagely beating Jesse destroy his car. They break the car windows and smash the fenders and hood with hammers and iron bars. They kill Jesse, put him back into his car in the front seat, and push the car into a three feet ravine along the side of the road to make it look like an accident. Jesse Fuller is dead.

1852 - 1919

JESSE'S 1930 ROLLS ROYCE

JESSE'S GRAVE

CHAPTER 28

THE CONCLUSION

At the age of 45, Carolina is blind because the bullet in his head has relocated to another area of the brain. He has memorized the whole bible and is a Sunday school teacher for children at Mt. Mariah Baptist Church. He enjoys going to church every Sunday to teach.

Clifton decides that he doesn't want to be a teacher after graduating from college. He loves trains and decides to become a train porter. He and his wife have twelve children and are happy living the house that Jackson gave to them.

Charlie, Dudley, Ernest, John, Primus, and Rochelle continue to operate the family ranch. In memory of their pa, they decided to ride Clydesdale horses every day at work on the ranch.

All of Jackson's daughters, Alice, Dilsie, Mimie, Gracie and Irene are teachers and are happily married. They continue to do the accounting for the family business.

Elida remarries. Her son by Jackson, Roy, died at an early age from pneumonia while away at school. Their daughter, Ola V., got married. Shortly after having a baby, she was shot in the head and killed by her step father, Elida's husband.

The legacy of Rev. Carolina Fuller and Jackson Fuller is alive and well in Louisiana.

Mt. Mariah Baptist Church celebrated its 152st anniversary in 2012. Pastor Fredrick Fuller, Bishop Jackson's great-great grandson, was appointed the new Pastor of Mt. Mariah in 2011. Prior to being appointed, he was the pastor of Antioch Baptist Church, the third church founded and built by his great-great-great grandfather, Rev. Carolina Fuller. Pastor Fredrick Fuller is the first Fuller to pastor Mt. Mariah Baptist Church since the death of Bishop Jackson Fuller, 93 years ago.

Pastor Fredrick Fuller

1852 - 1919

In paraphrasing Ecclesiastes 1:9, **"What was shall be again,"** Rightfully so, **PROVIDENCE** is at work again.

There is much similarity with Pastor Fredrick Fuller and Bishop Jackson Fuller. They were both pastors at one of the churches founded and built by Rev. Carolina Fuller prior to becoming the pastor of Mt. Mariah Baptist Church. Pastor Fredrick Fuller is strongly connected to God like Bishop Jackson was. I can confidently say that God's anointing is prevalent in his life. **He's an anointed man called by God to preach. (Thus saith the Lord, "Touch not mine anointed, and do my prophets no harm." Psalms 105:15)**

THIS UNTOLD SAGA HAS NOW BEEN TOLD

This story is not a documentary.

1852 - 1919

MT. MARIAH'S BAPTIST CHURCH
Life Center Building

MT. MARIAH BAPTIST CHURCH

INTERIOR

MT. MARIAH BAPTIST CHURCH

Made in the USA
Charleston, SC
27 November 2012